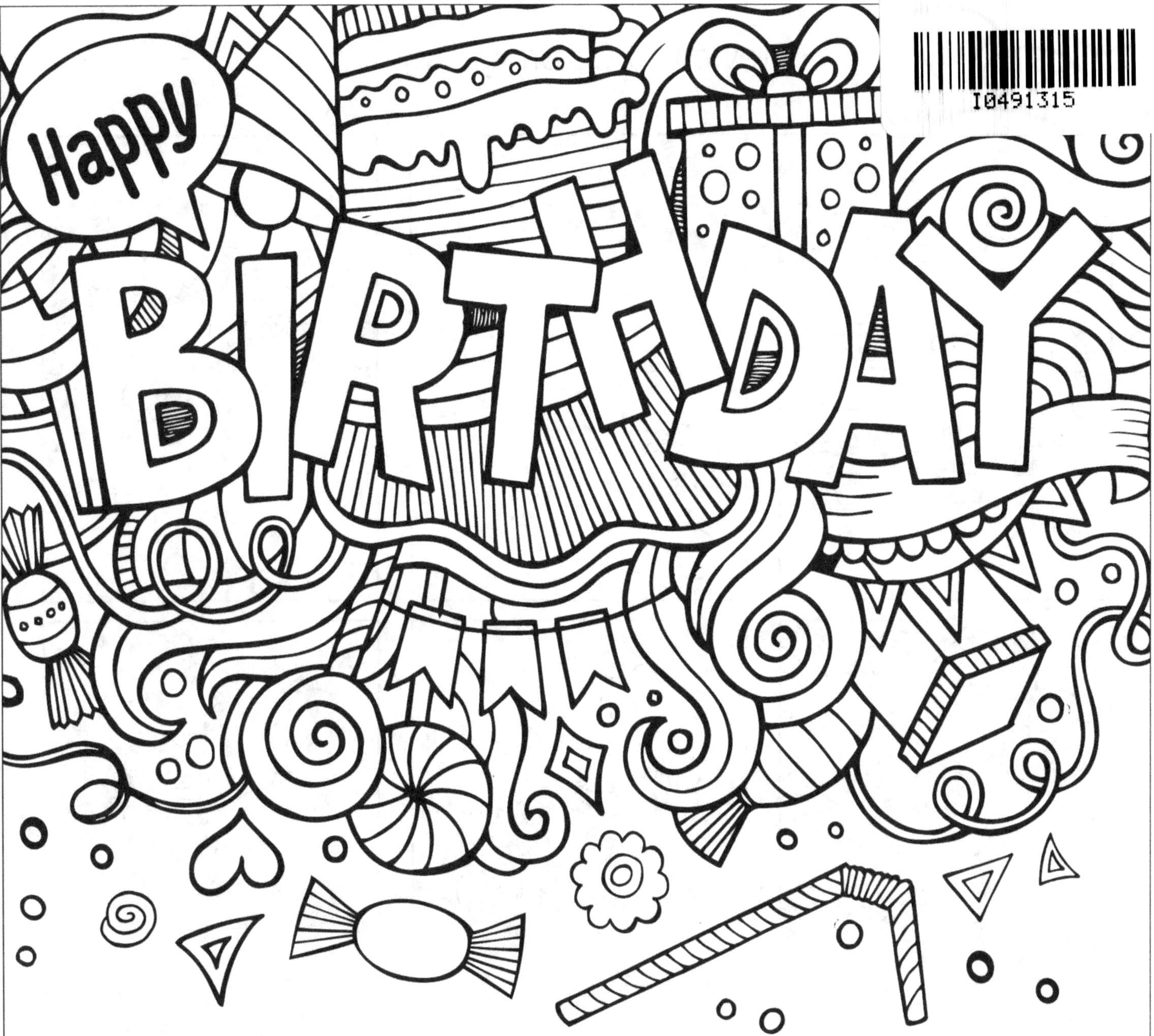

Anti-Stress Coloring Book

Happy Birthday Edition

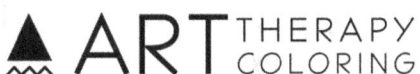
ART THERAPY COLORING

Preview of Coloring Pages

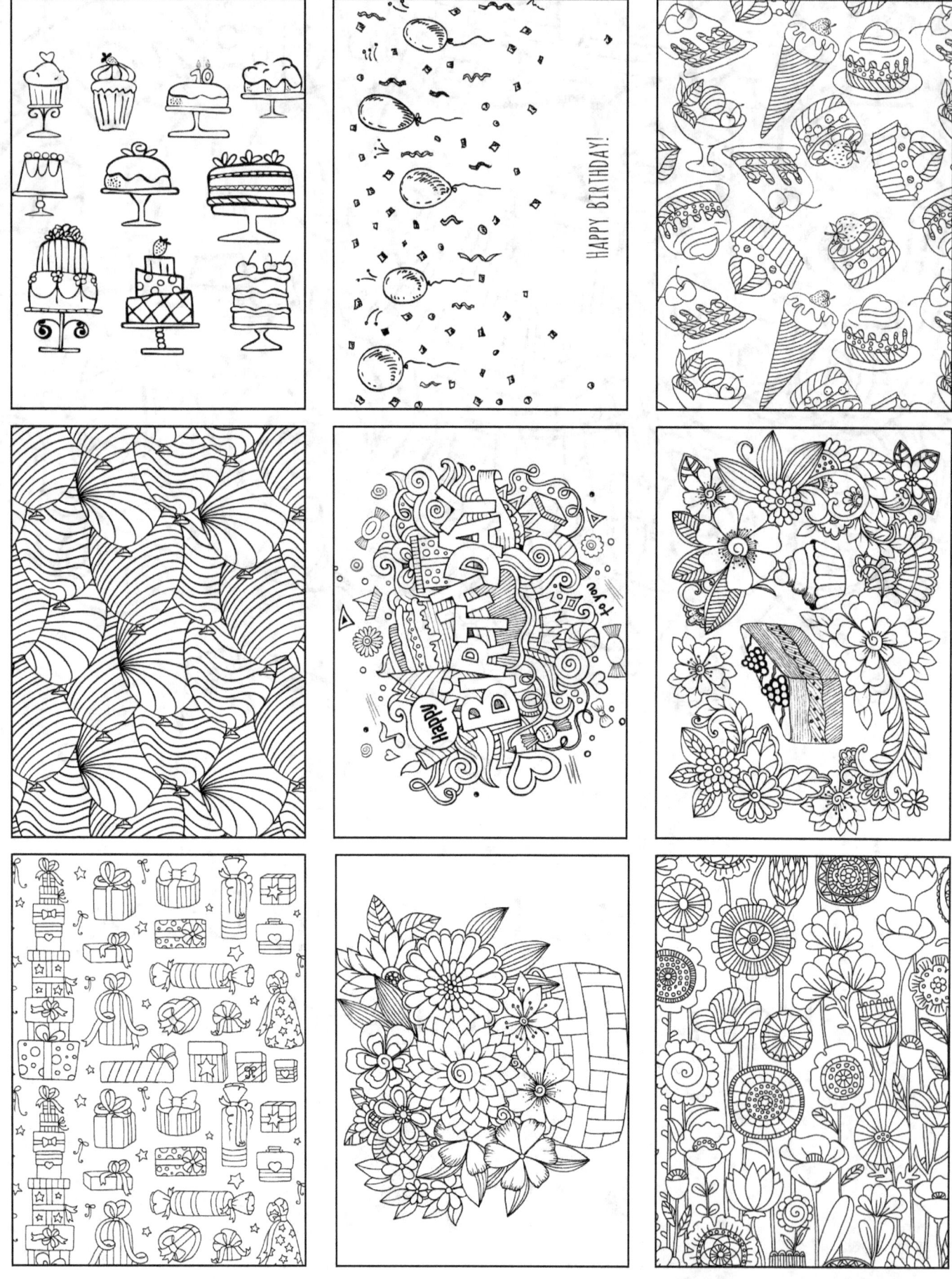

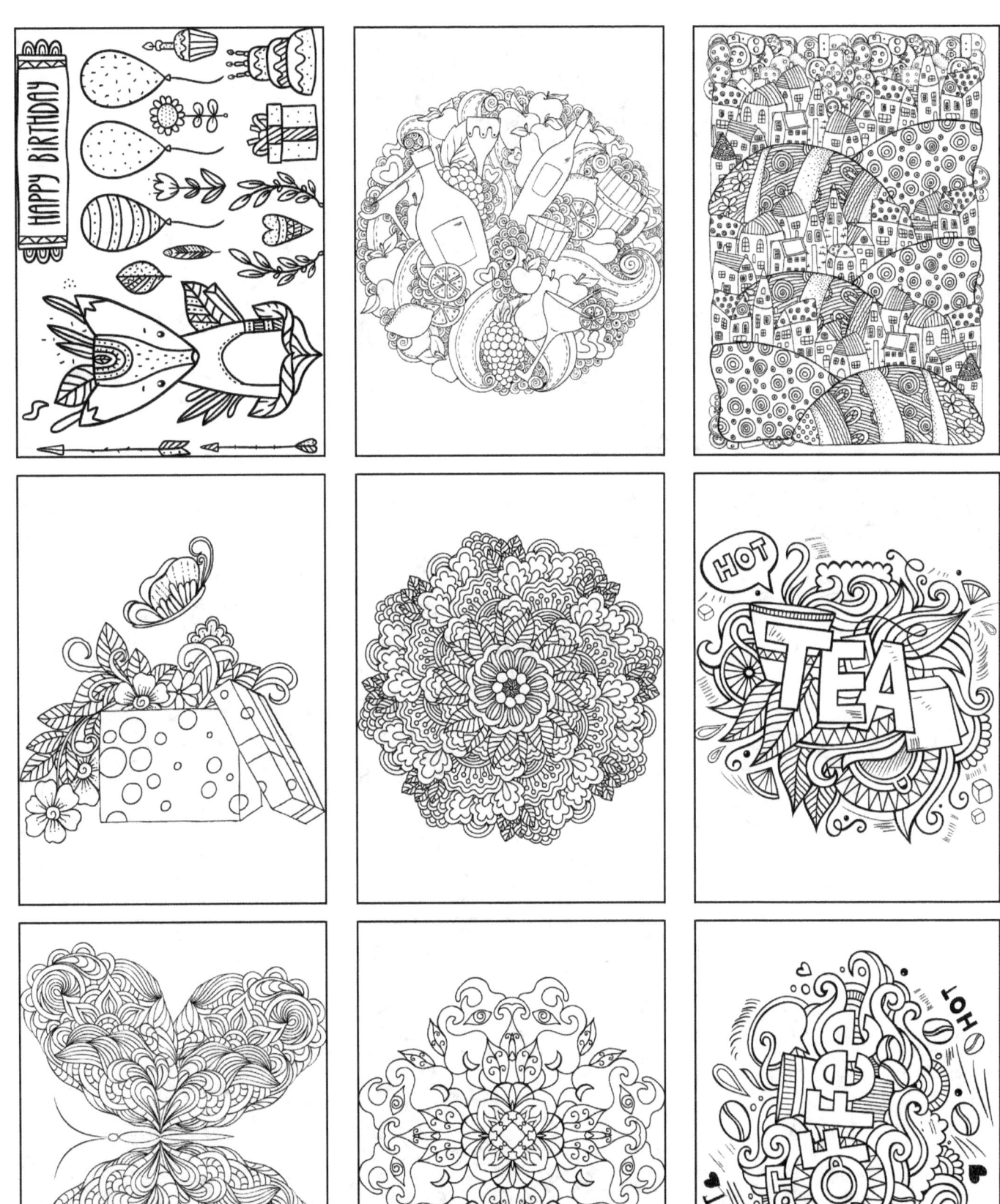

Preview of Coloring Pages

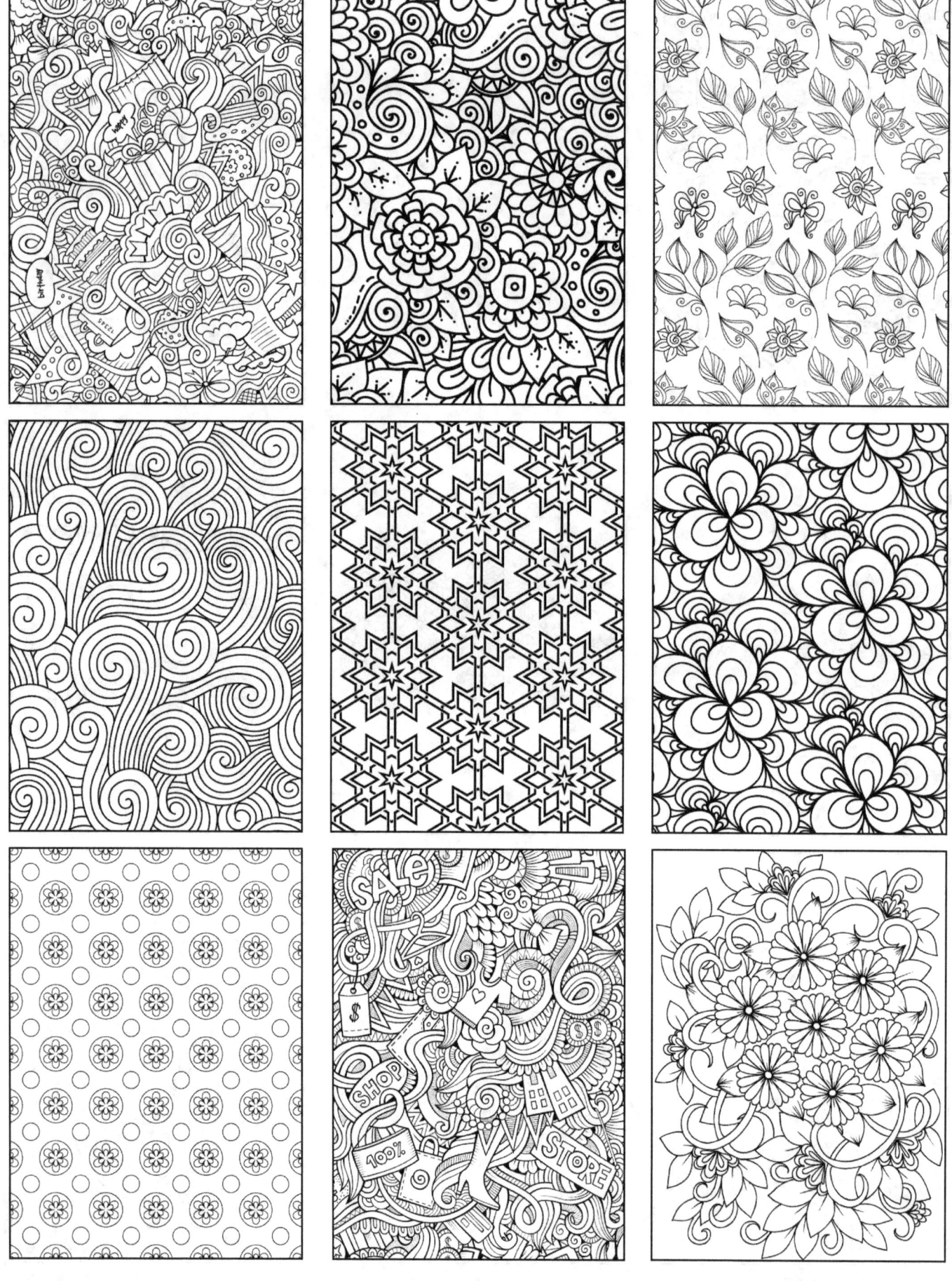

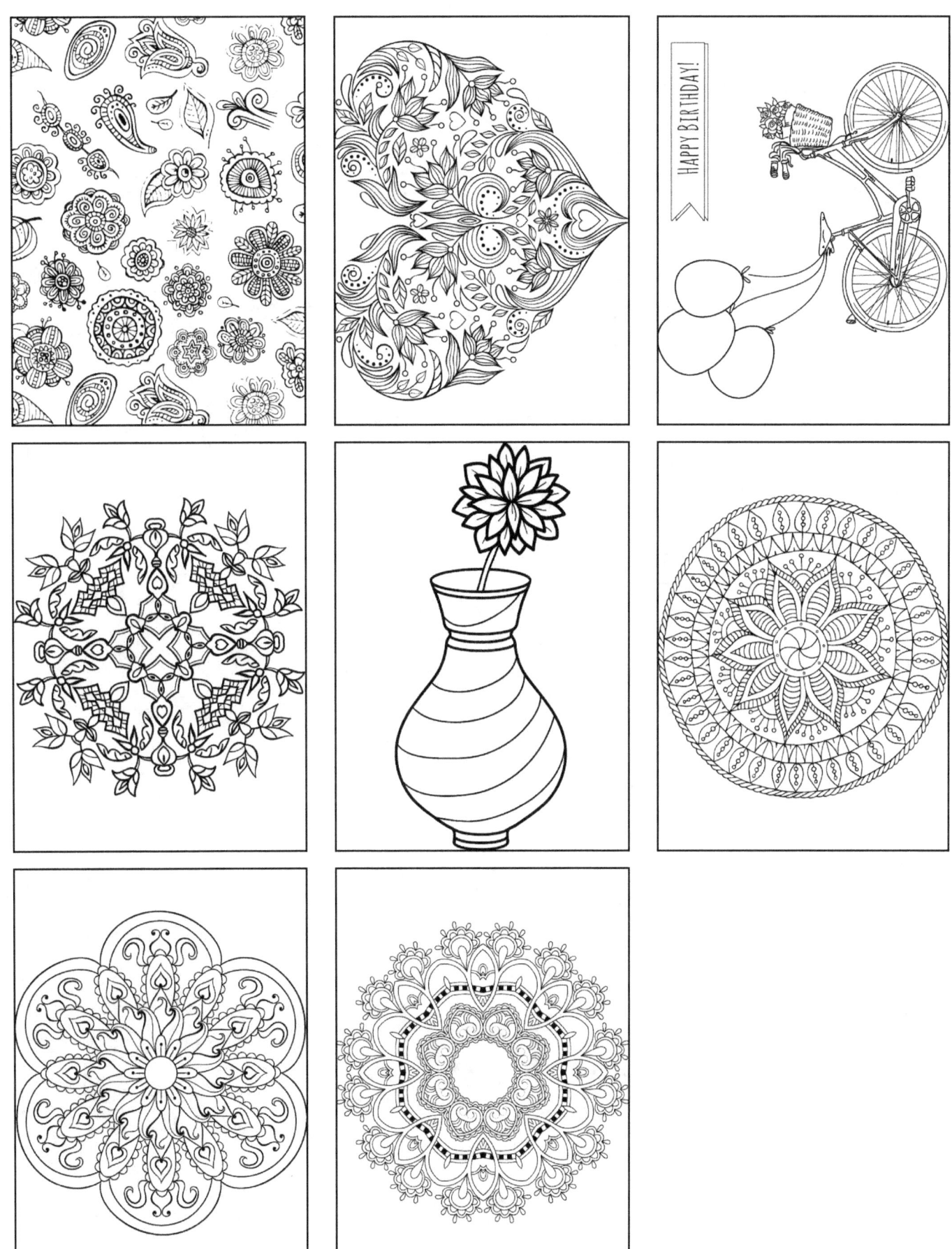

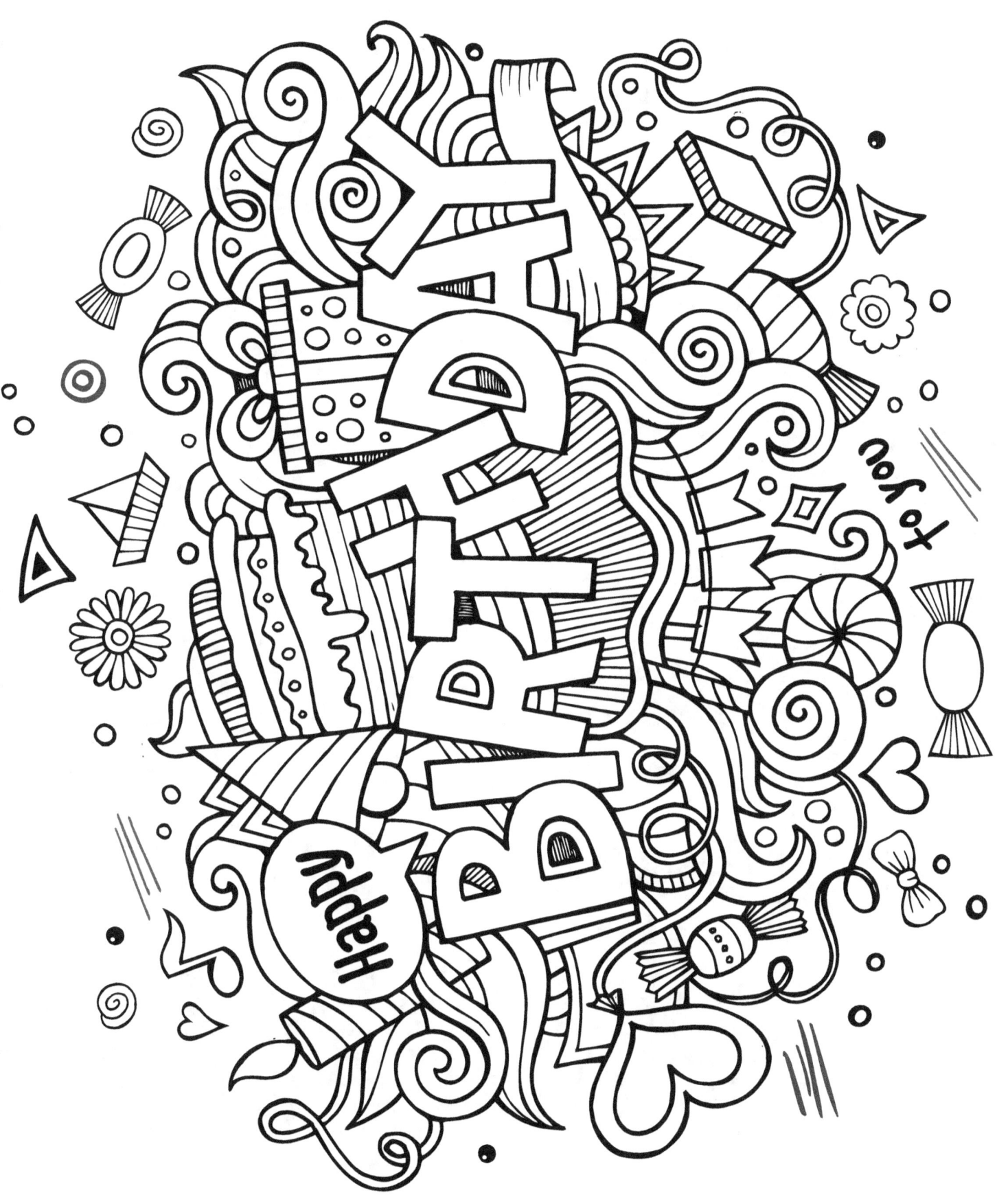

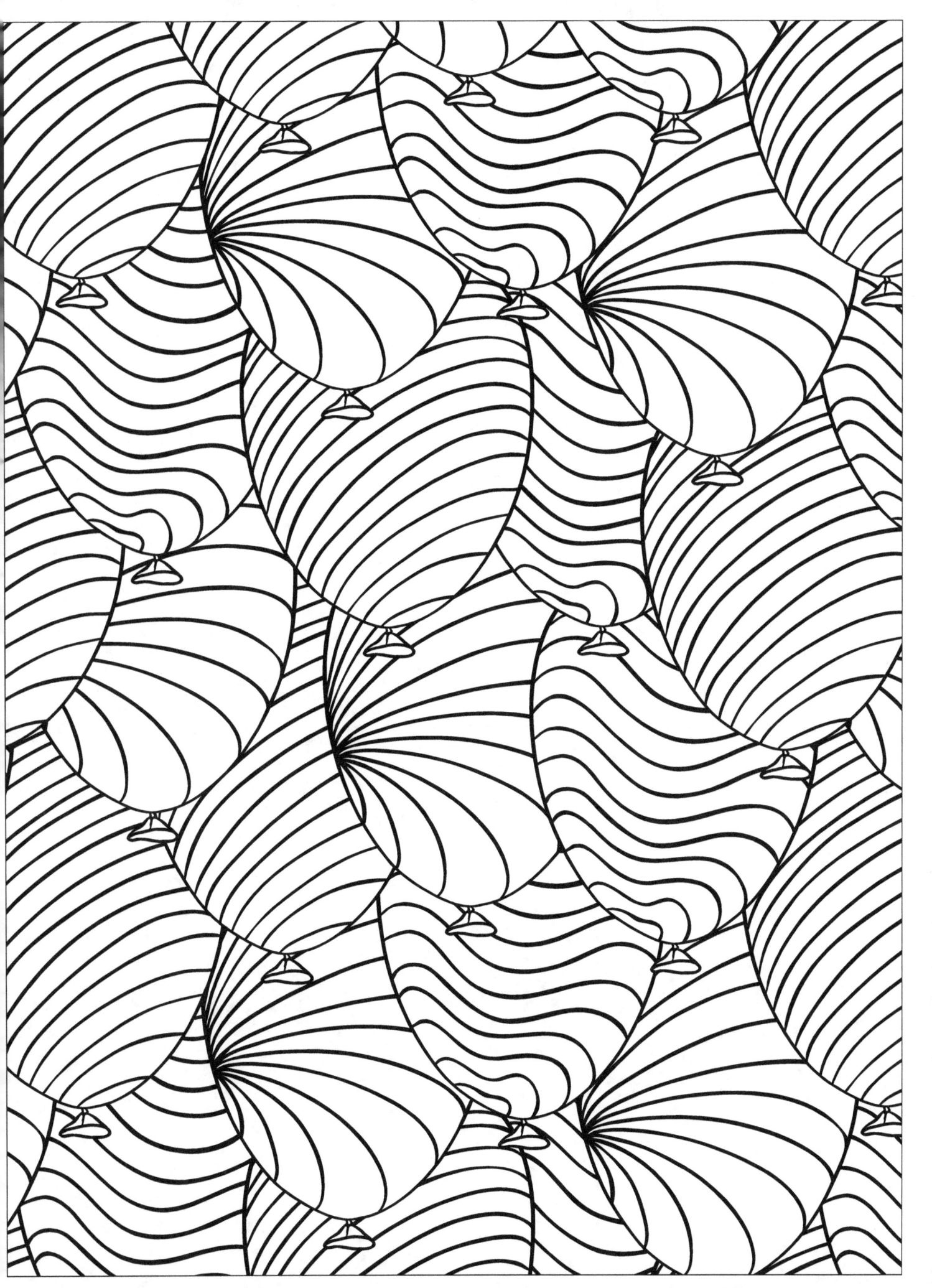

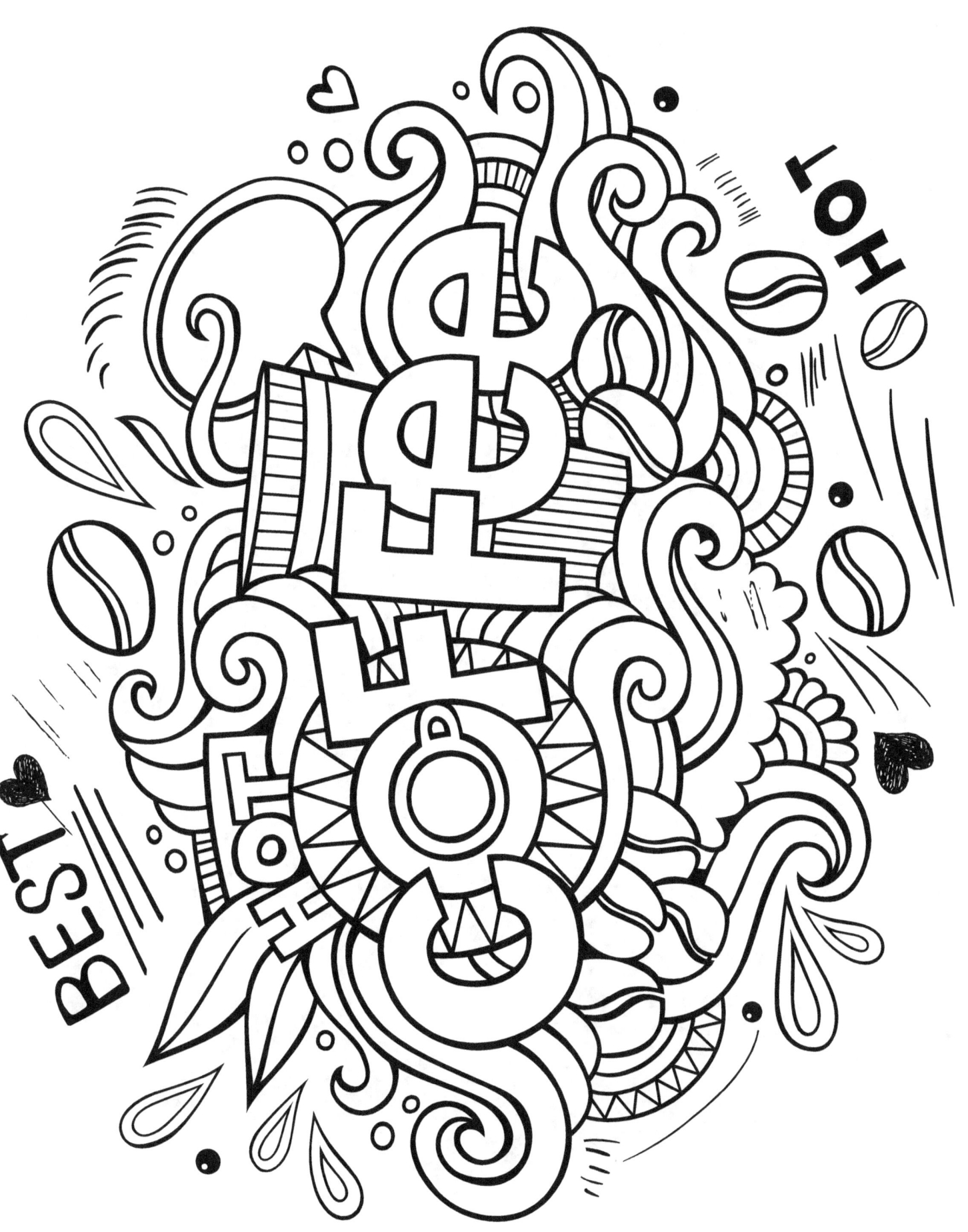

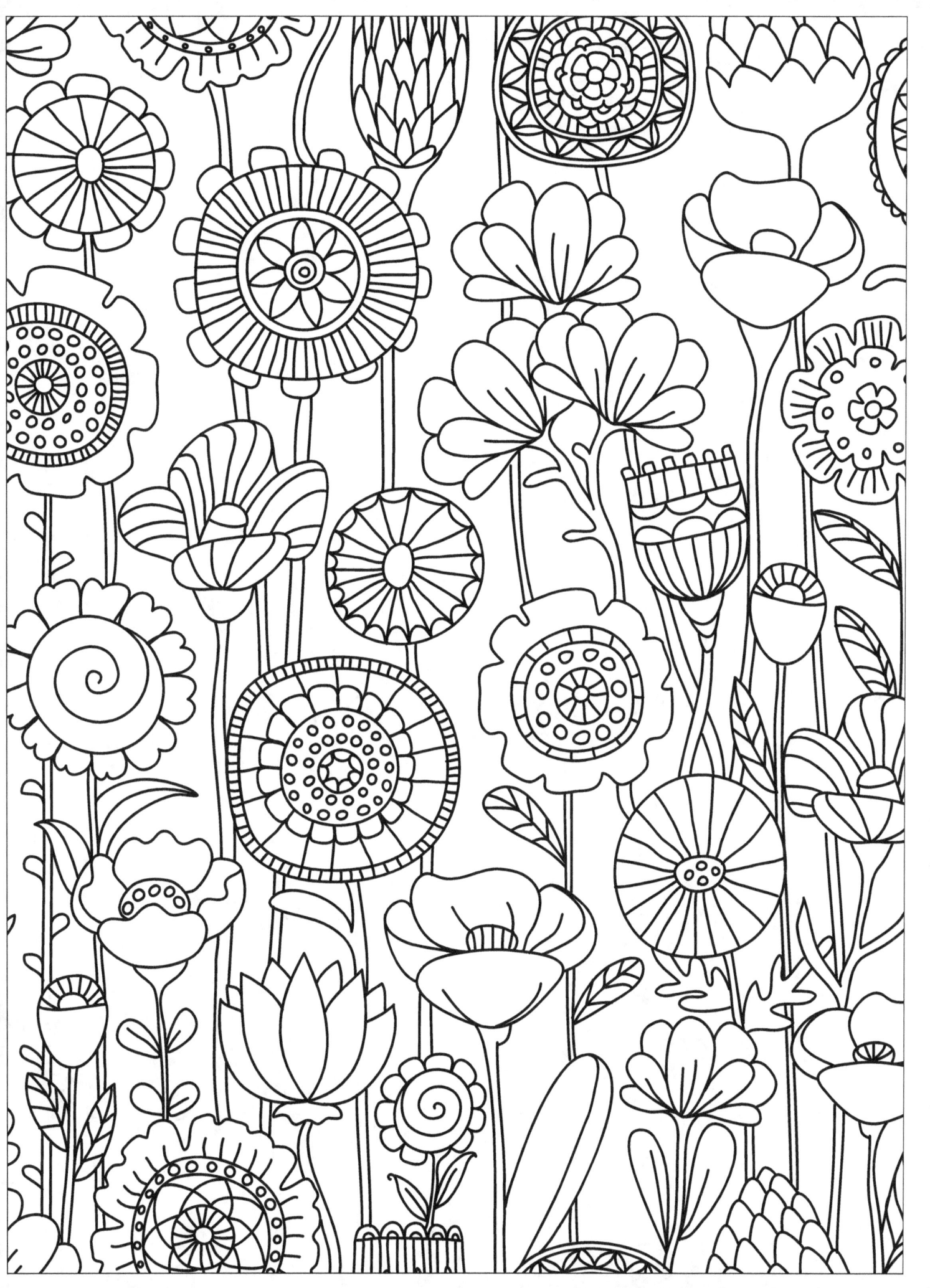

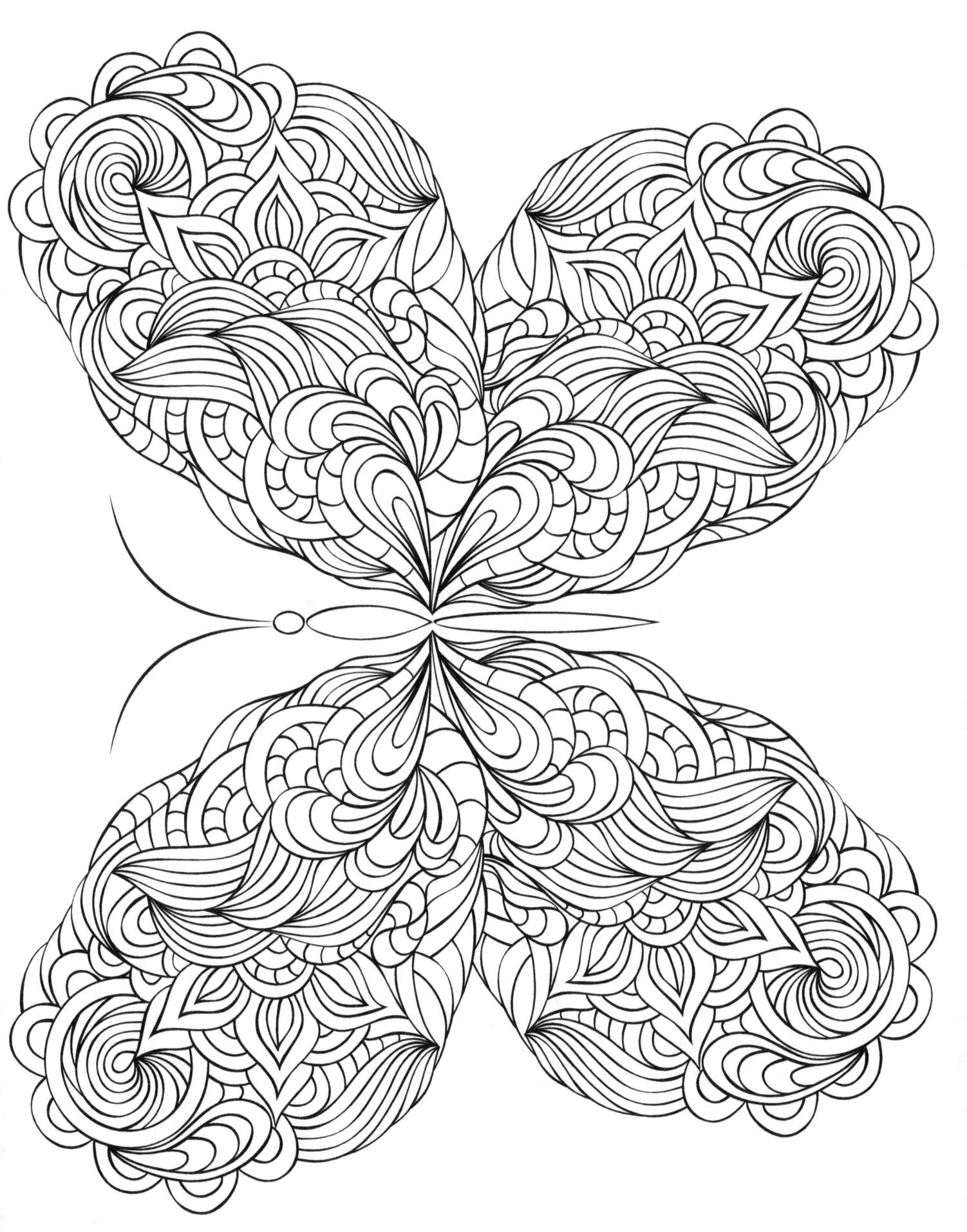

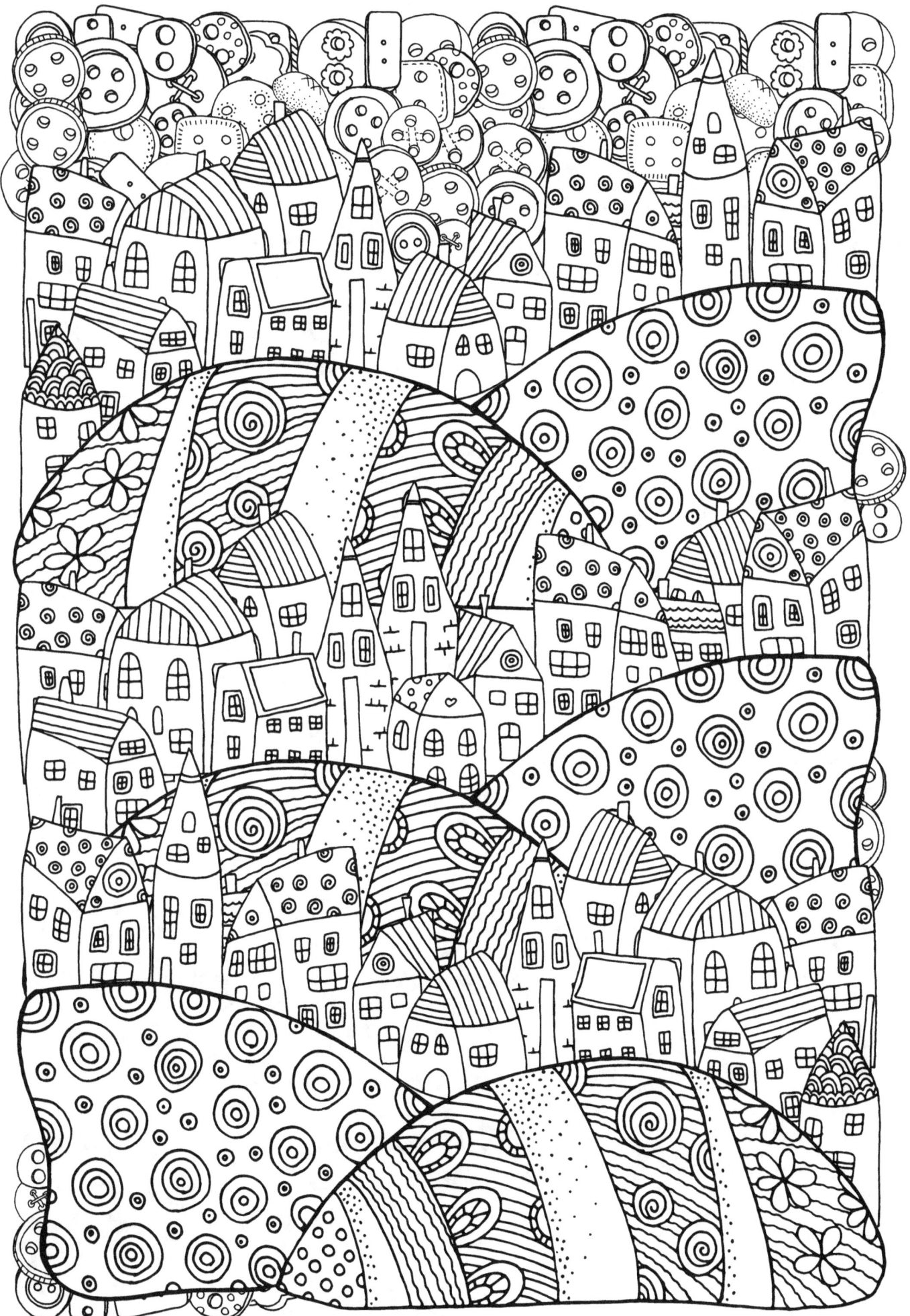

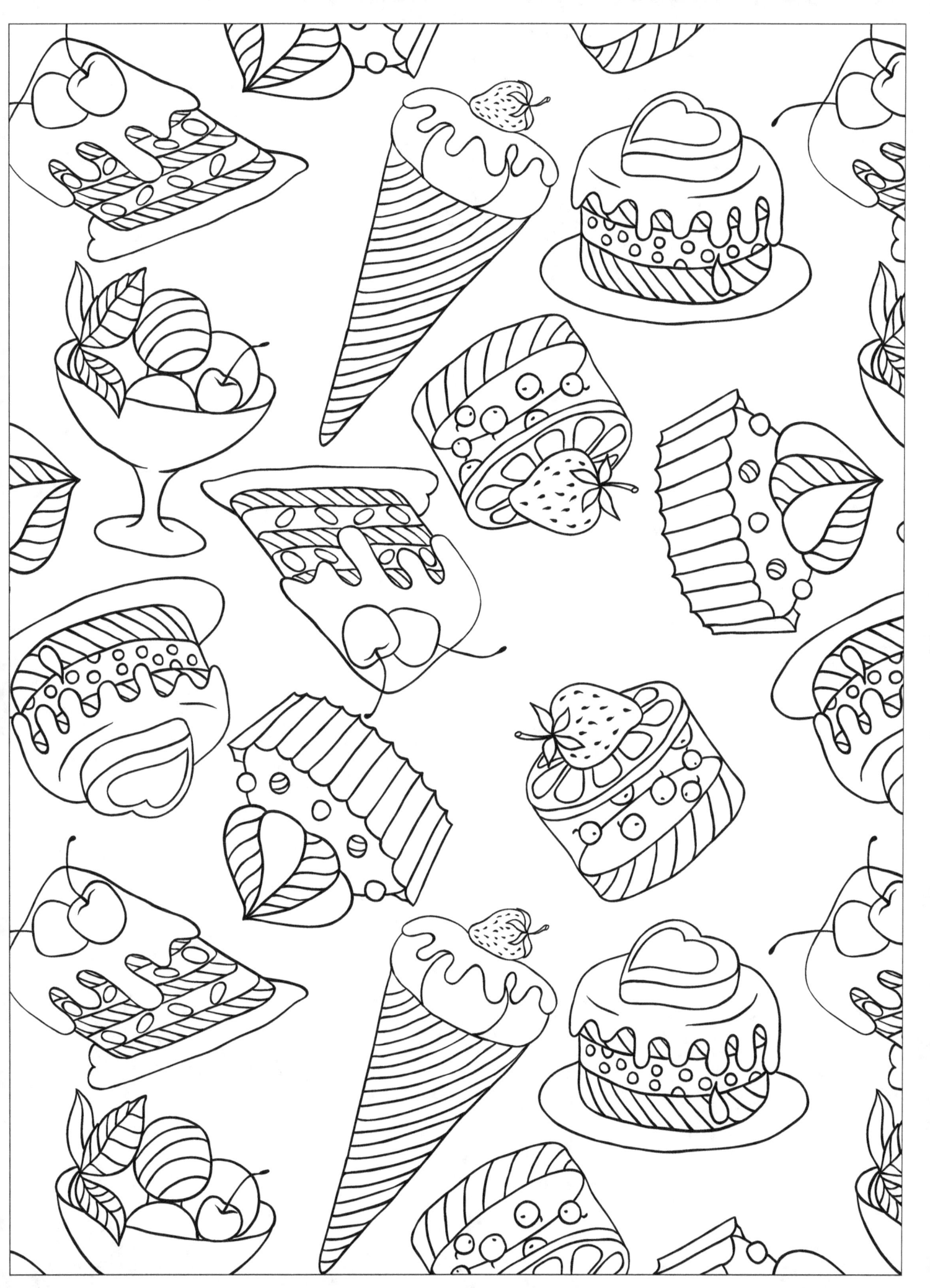

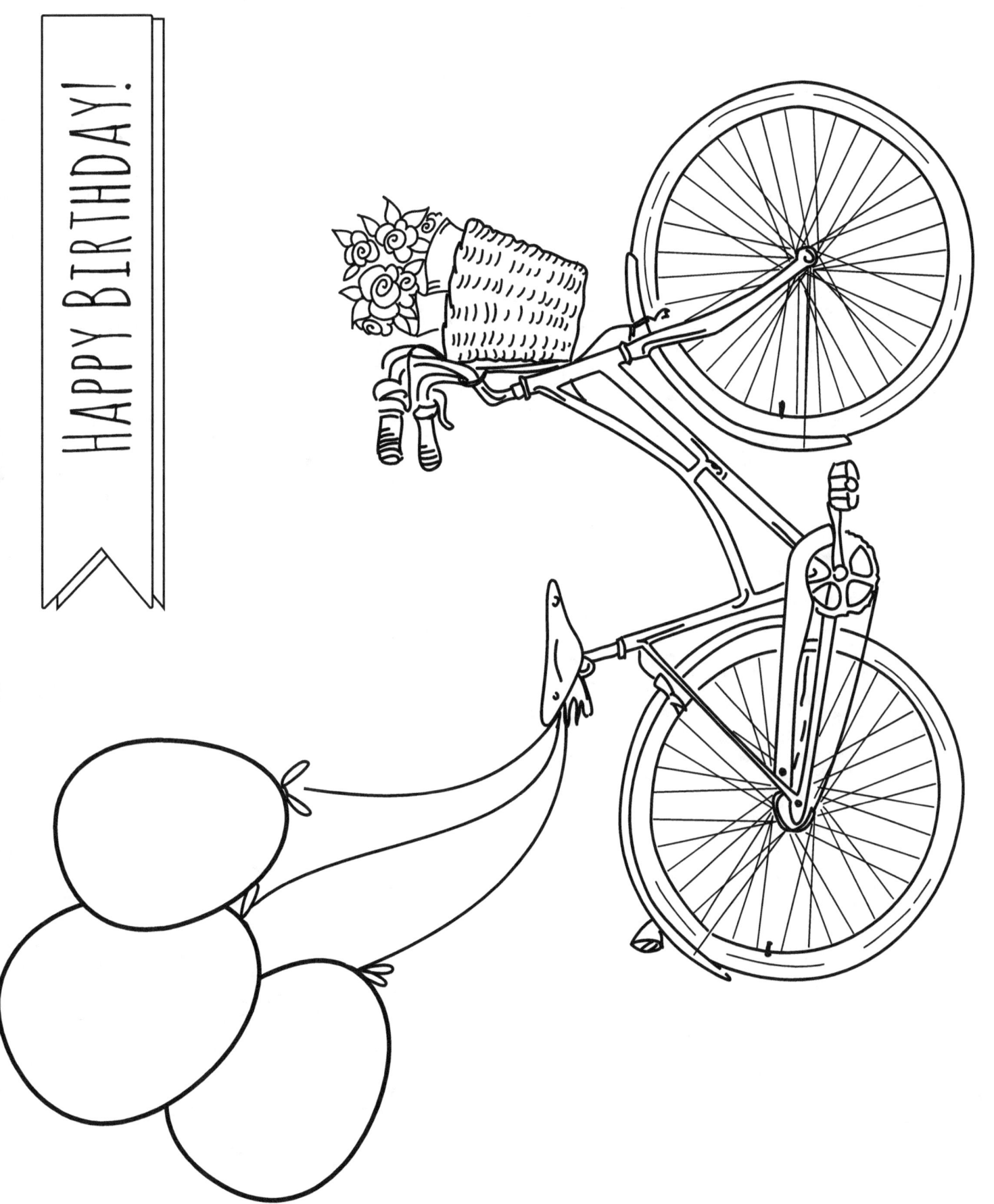

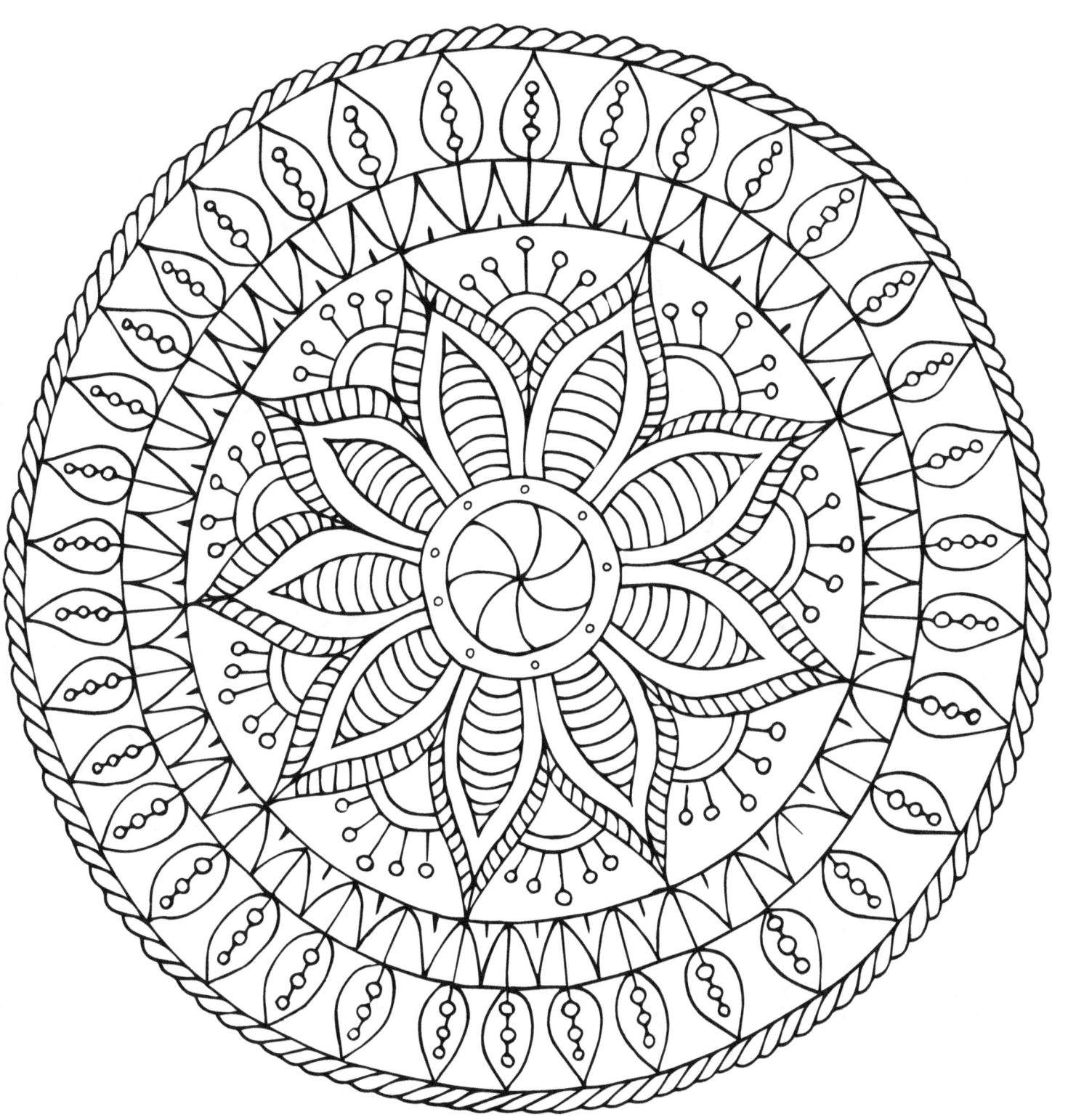

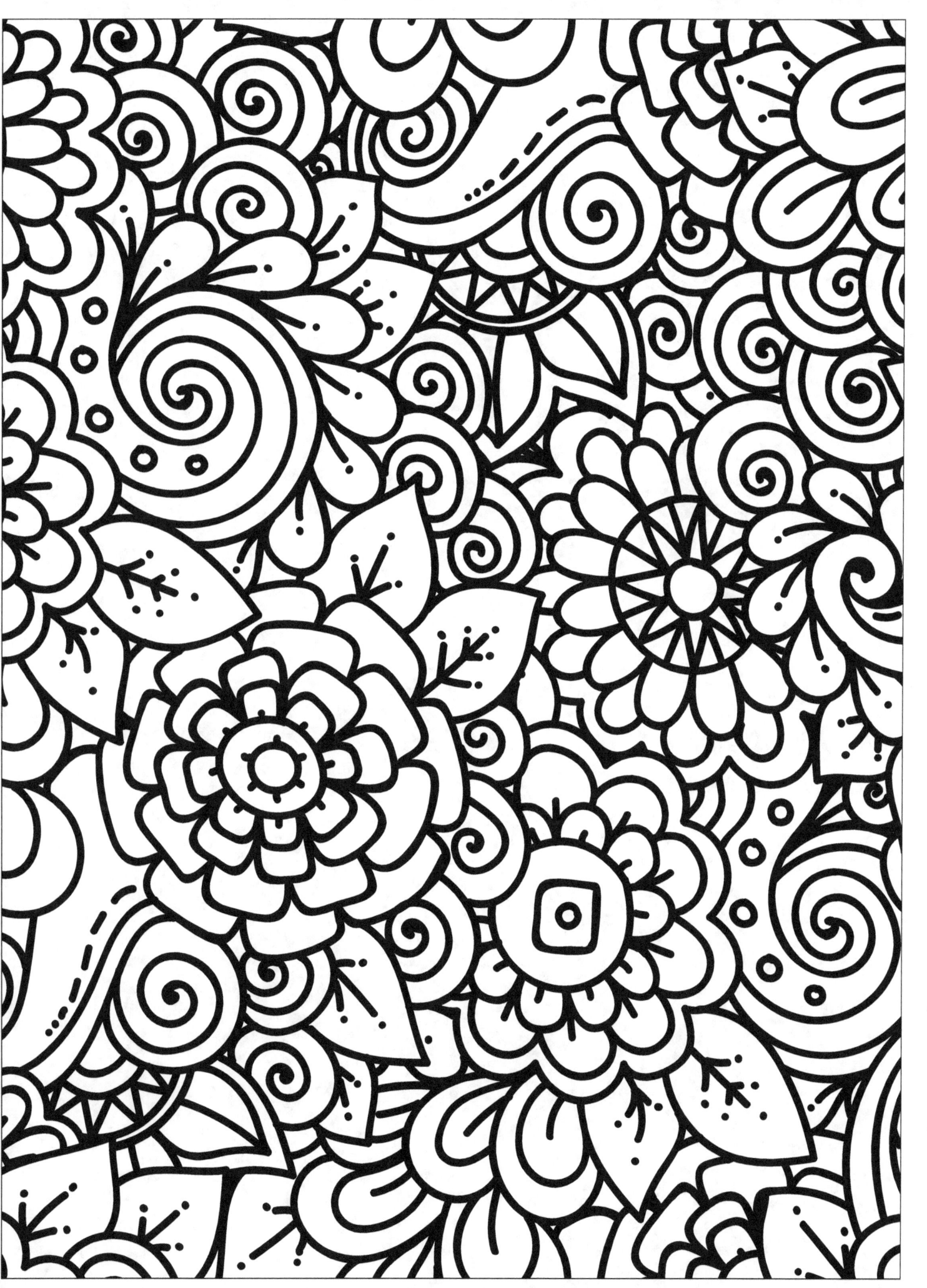

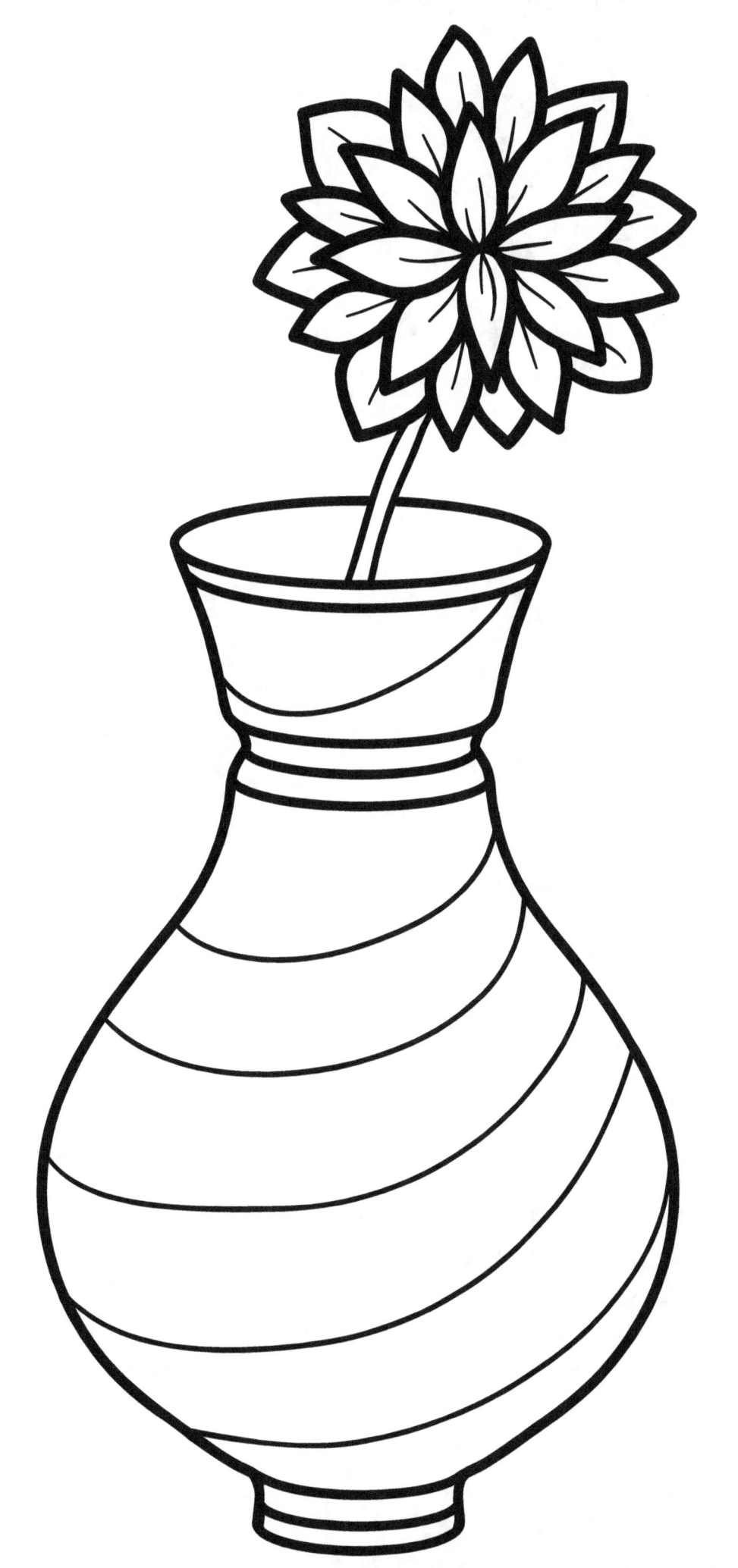

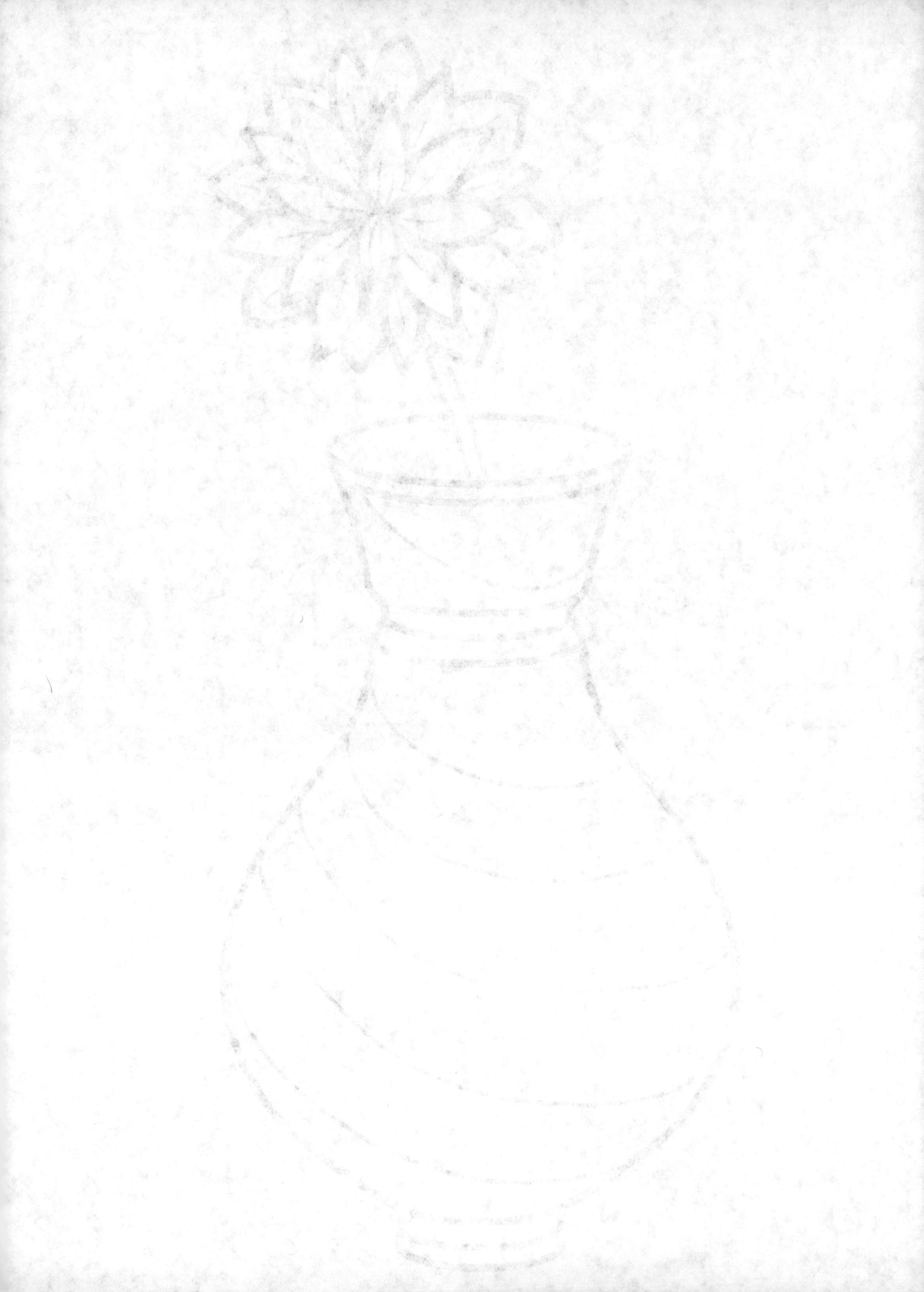

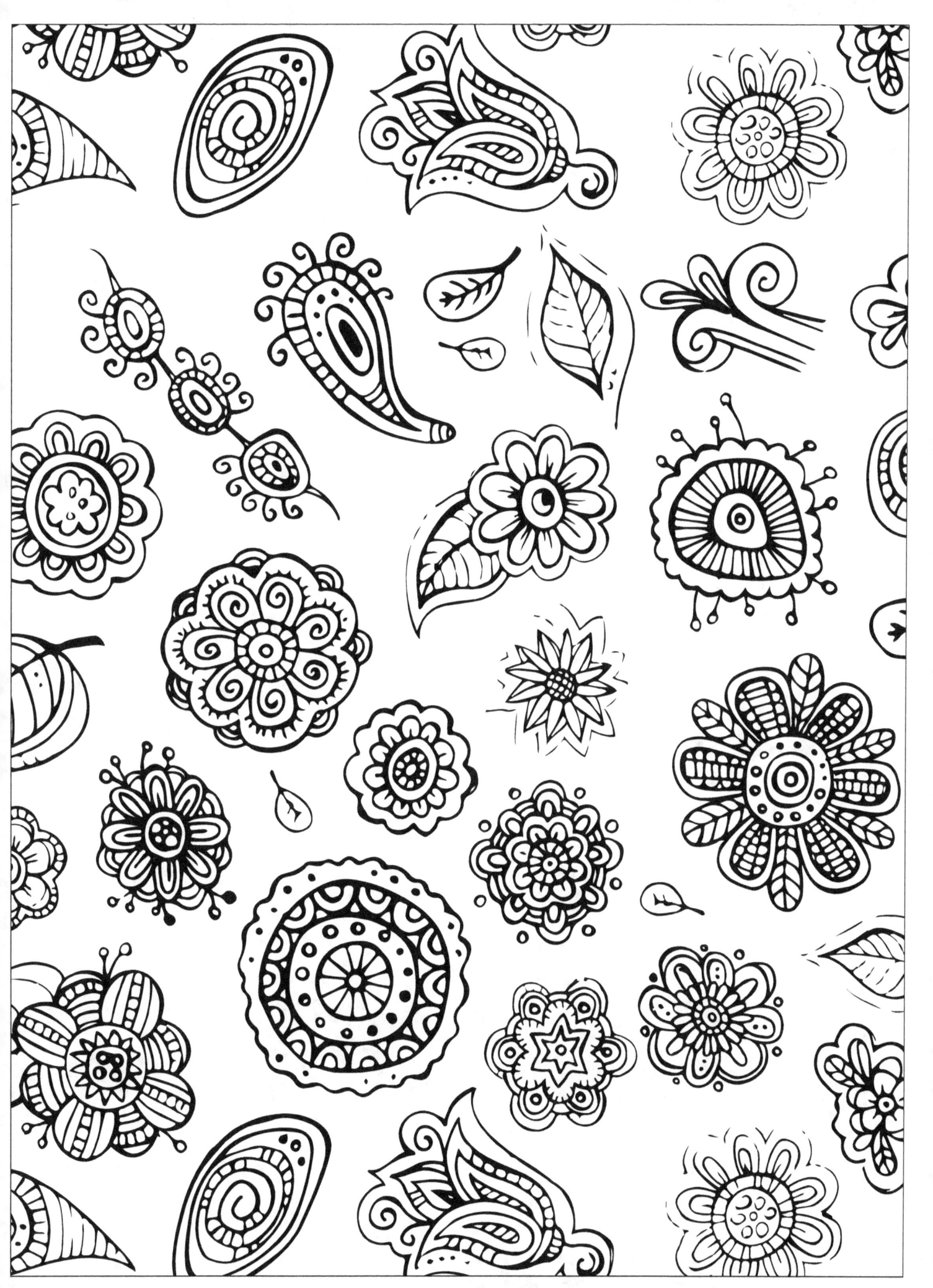

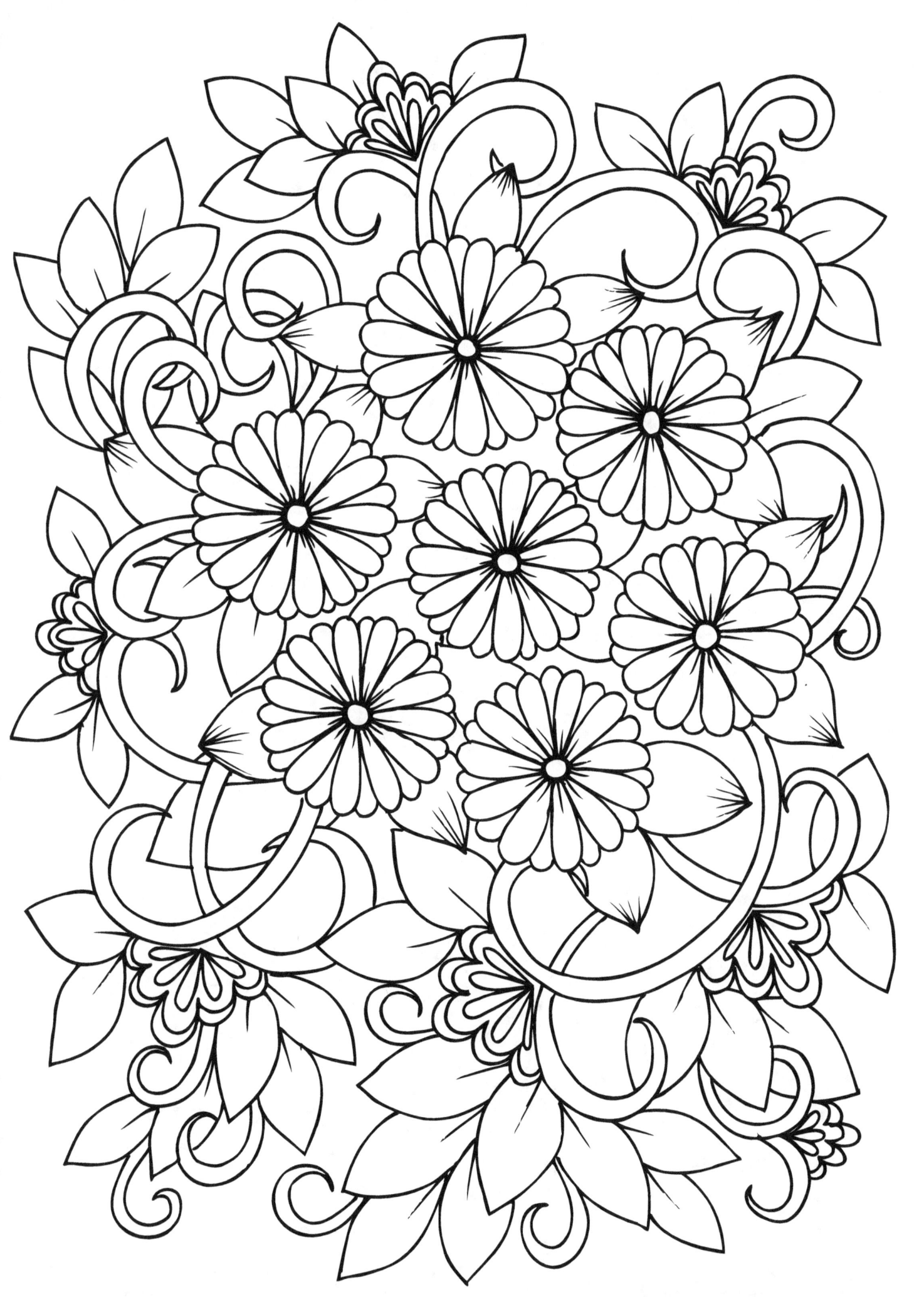

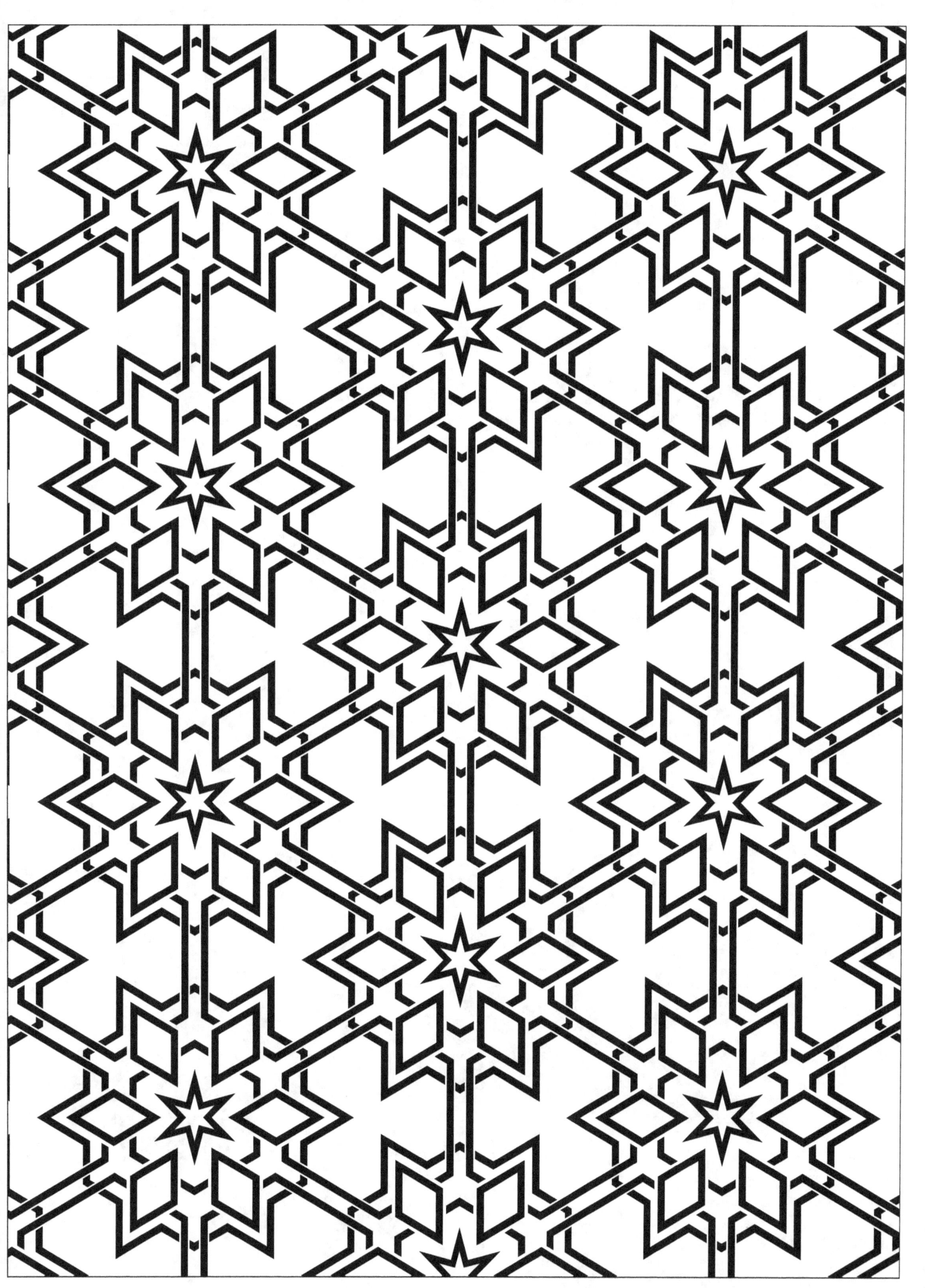

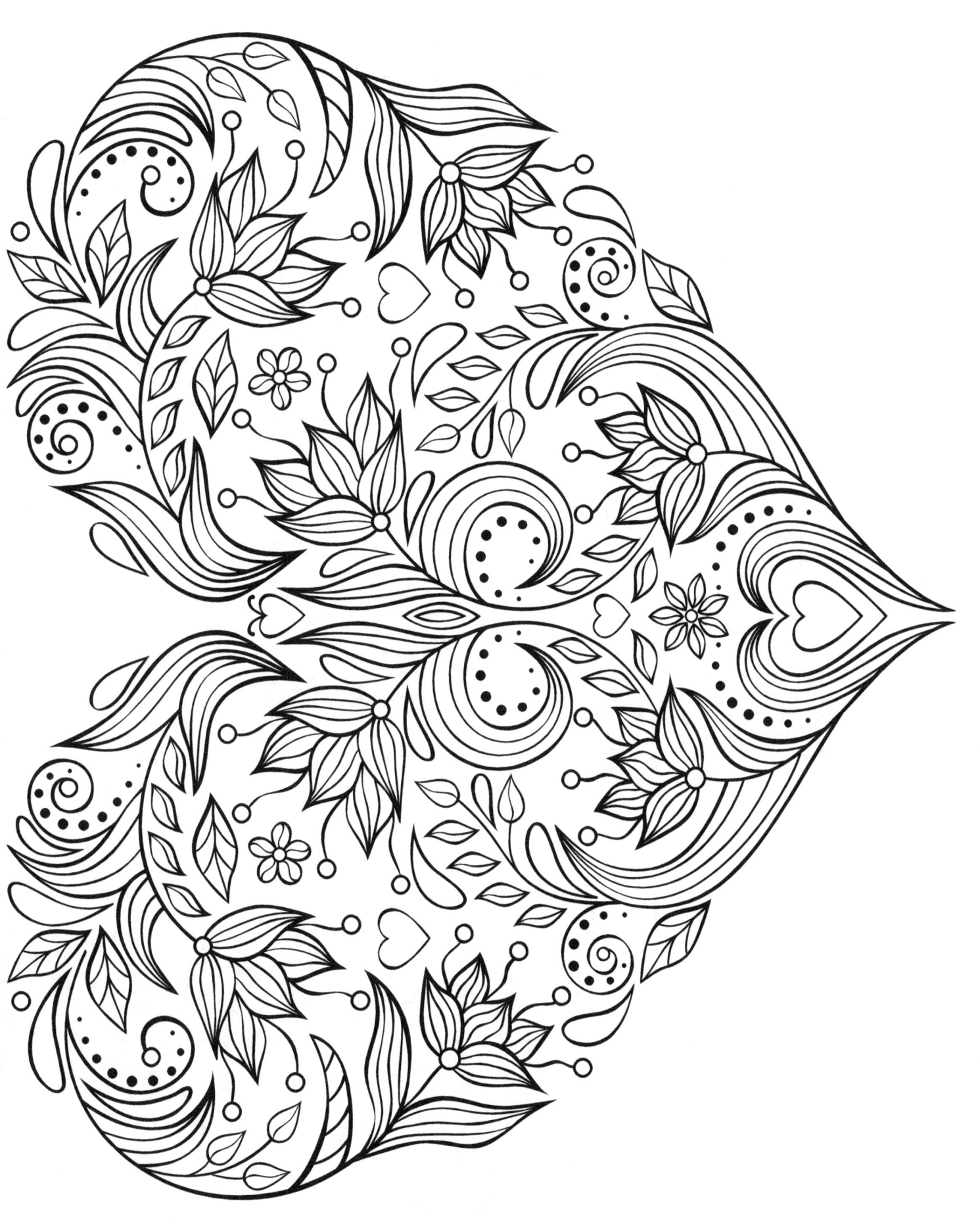

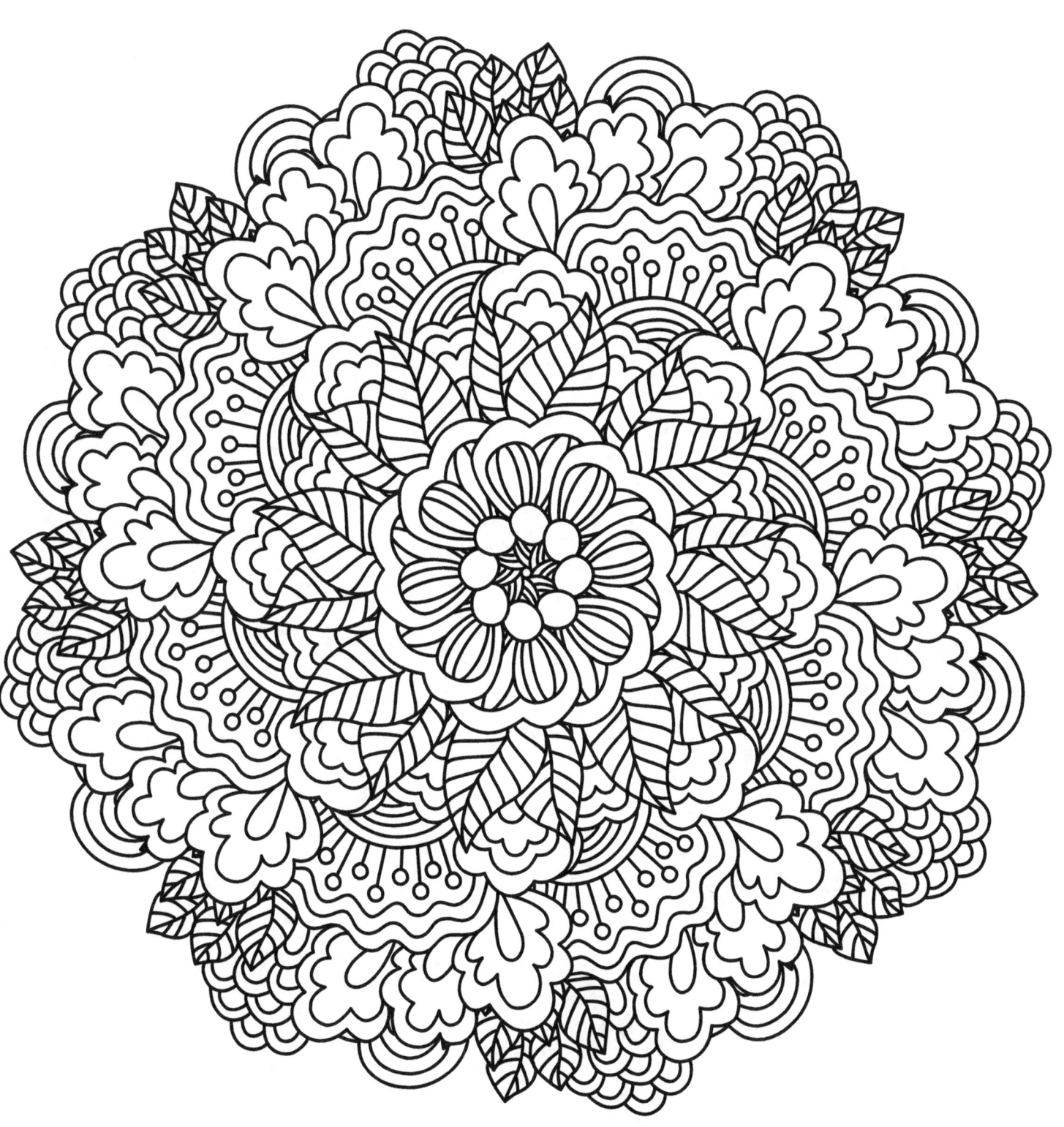

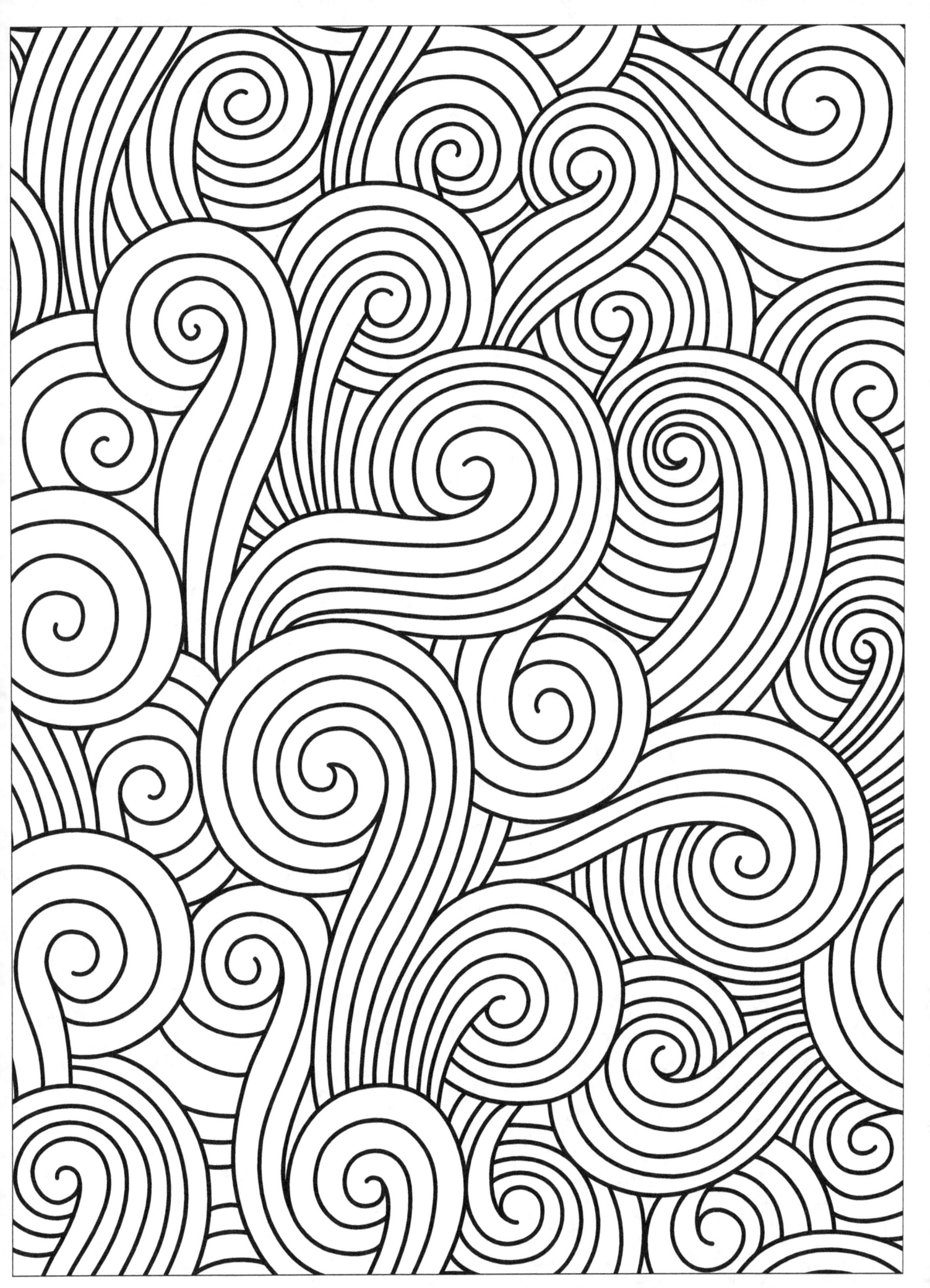

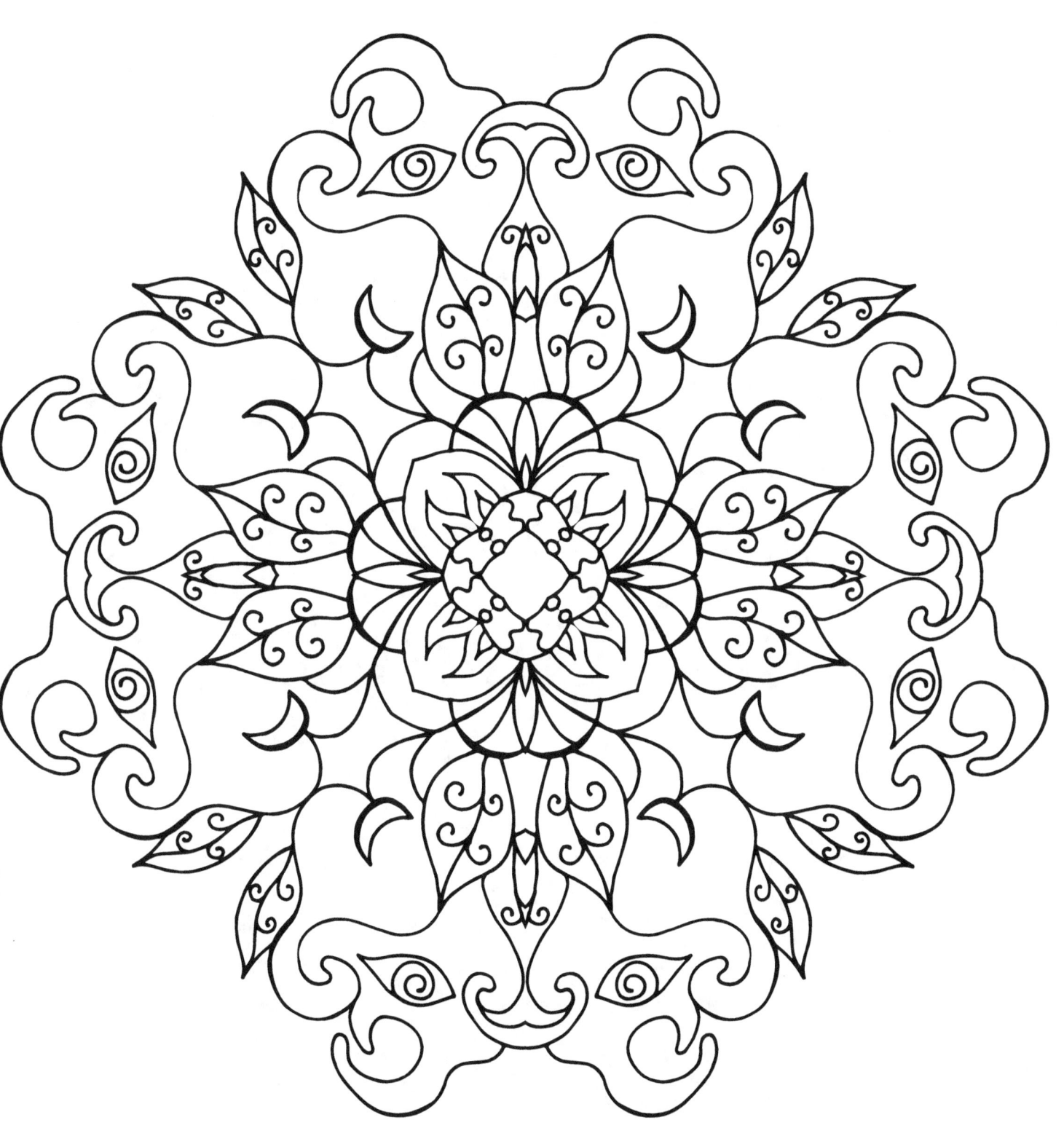

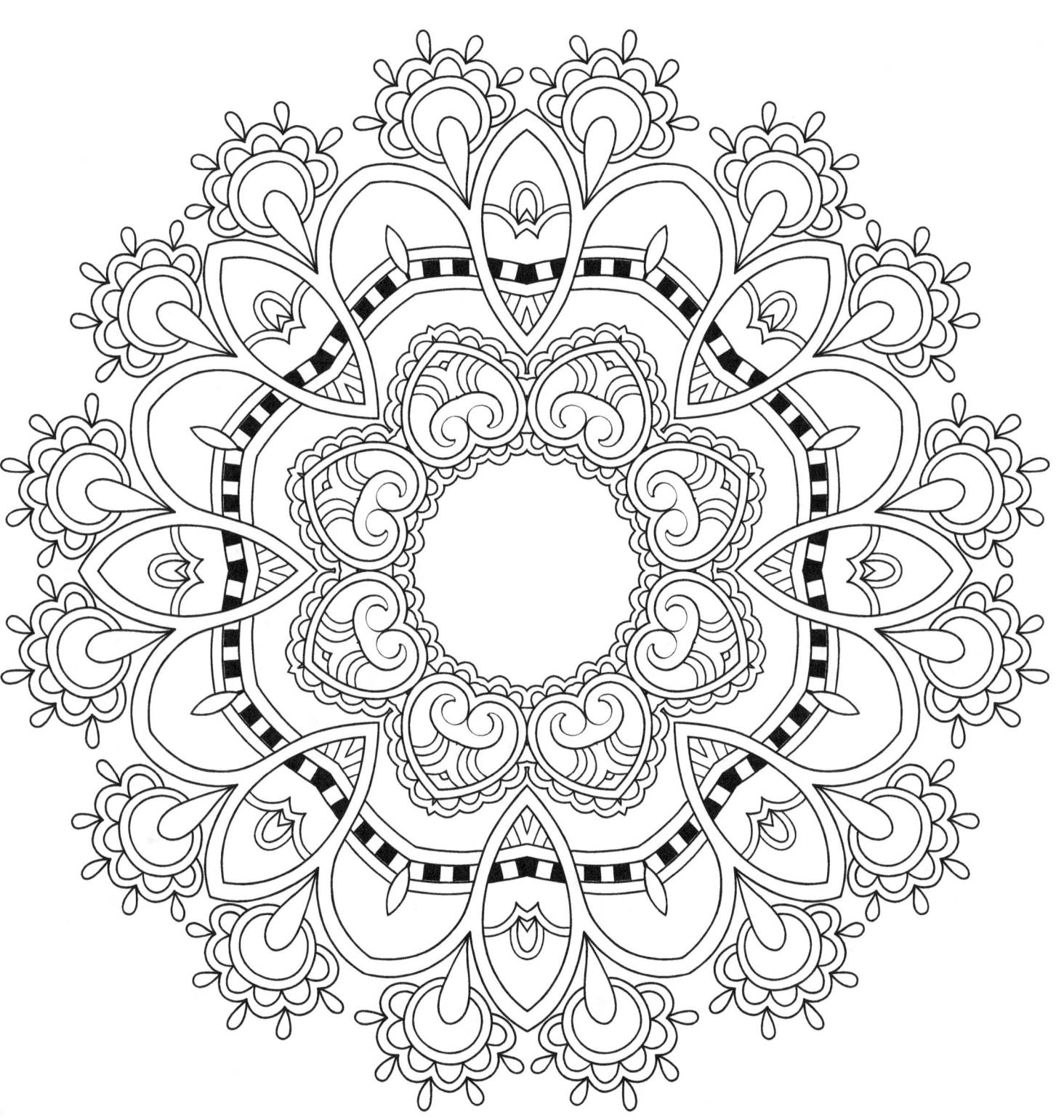

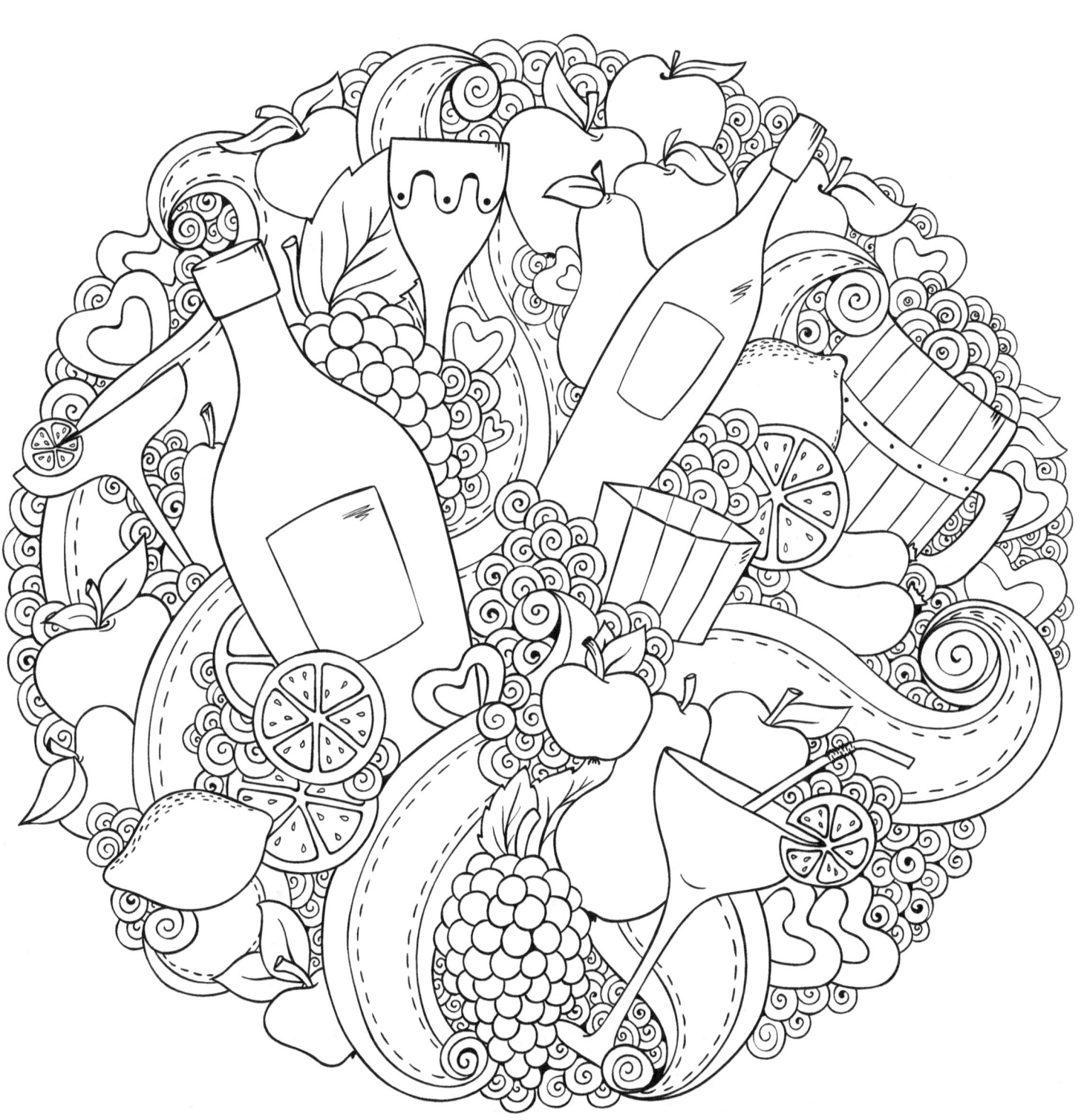

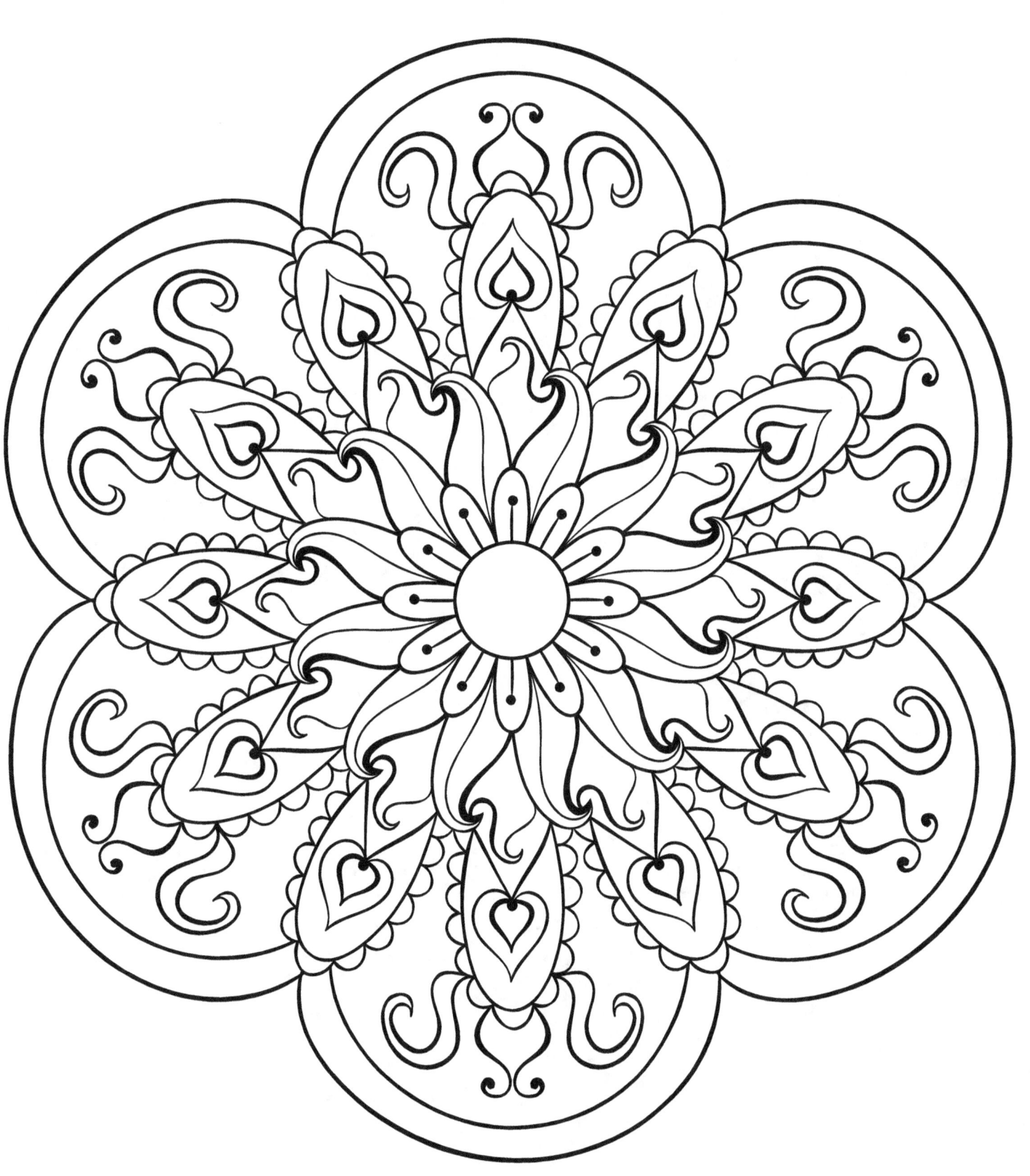

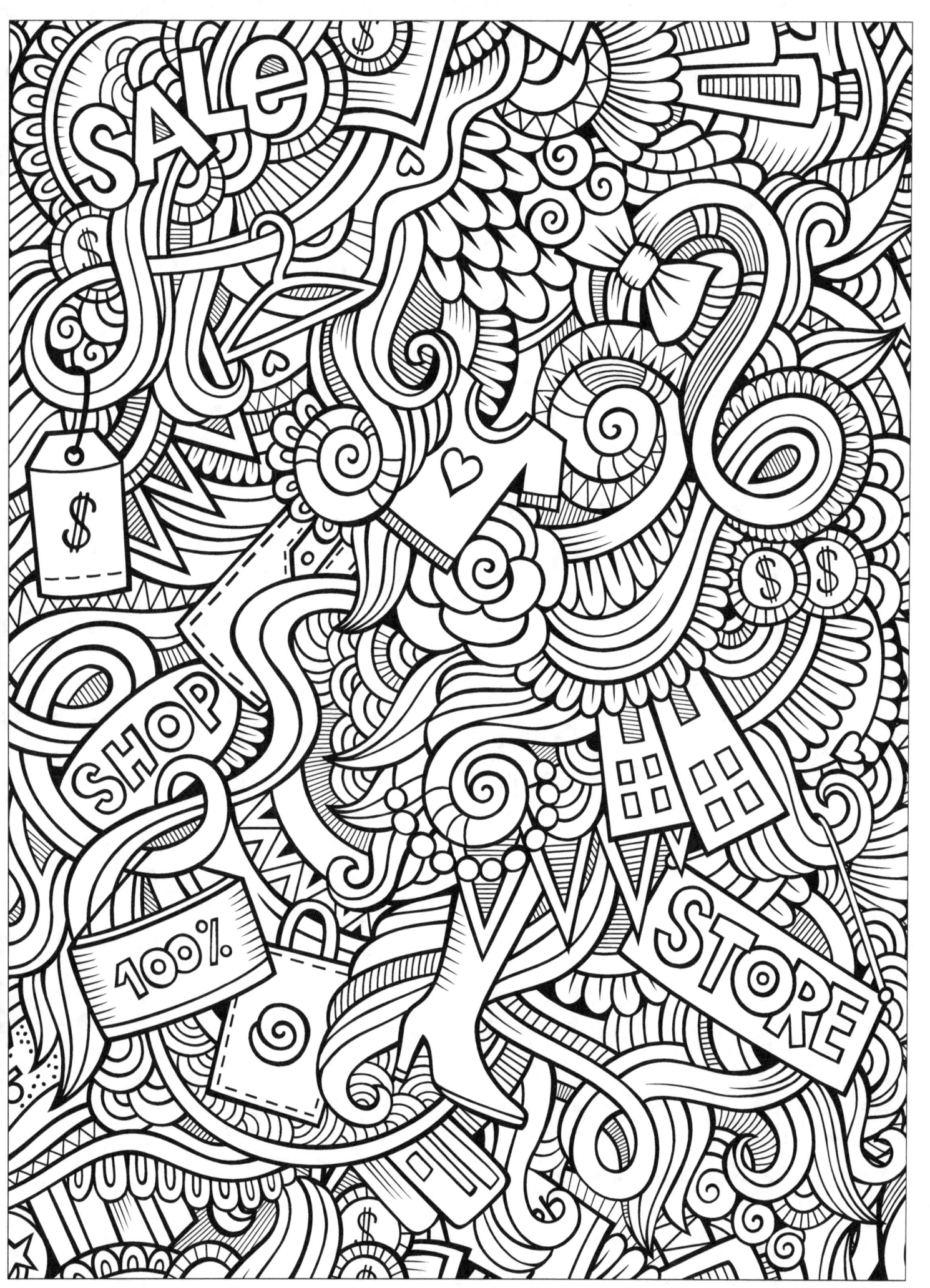

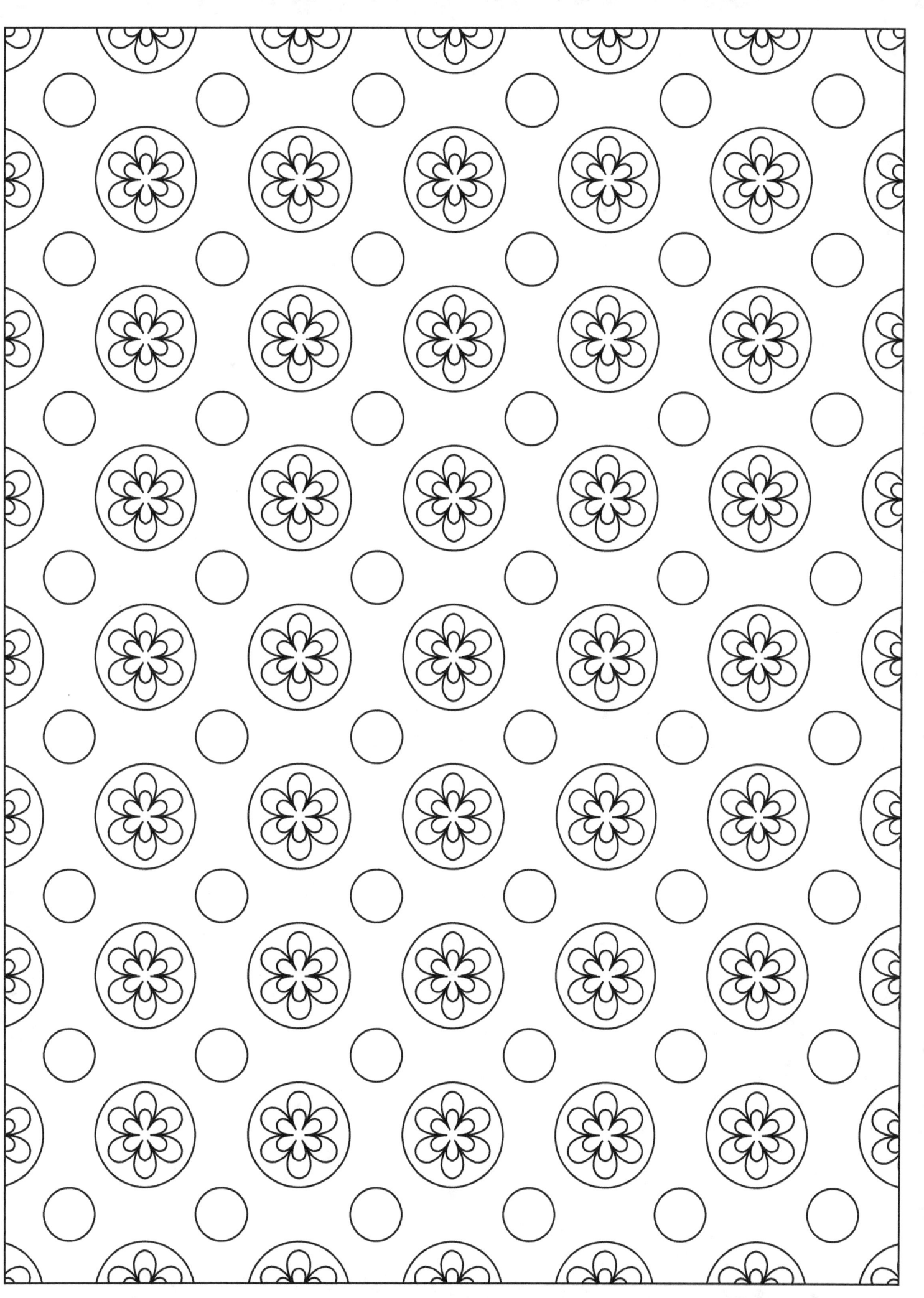

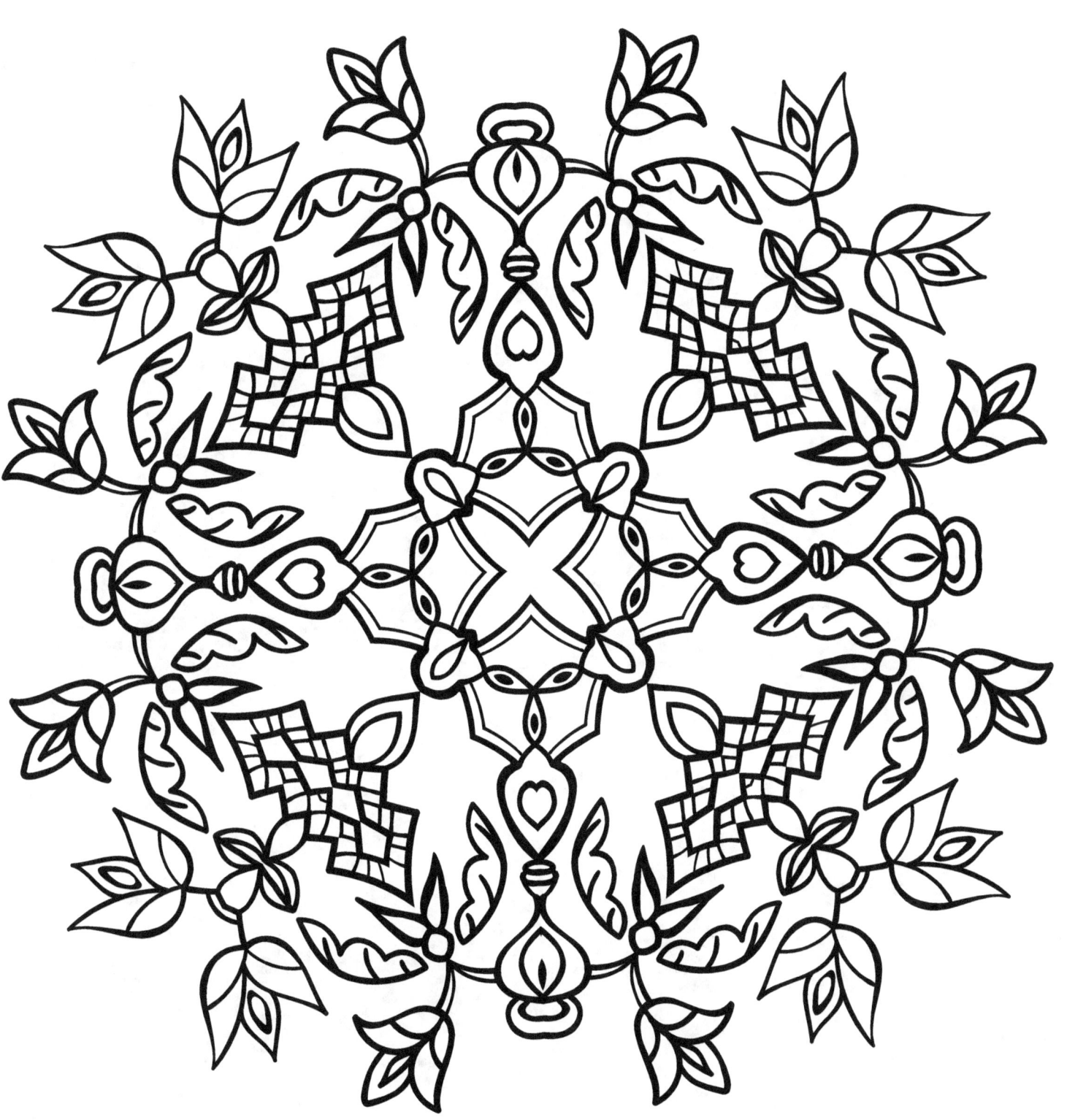

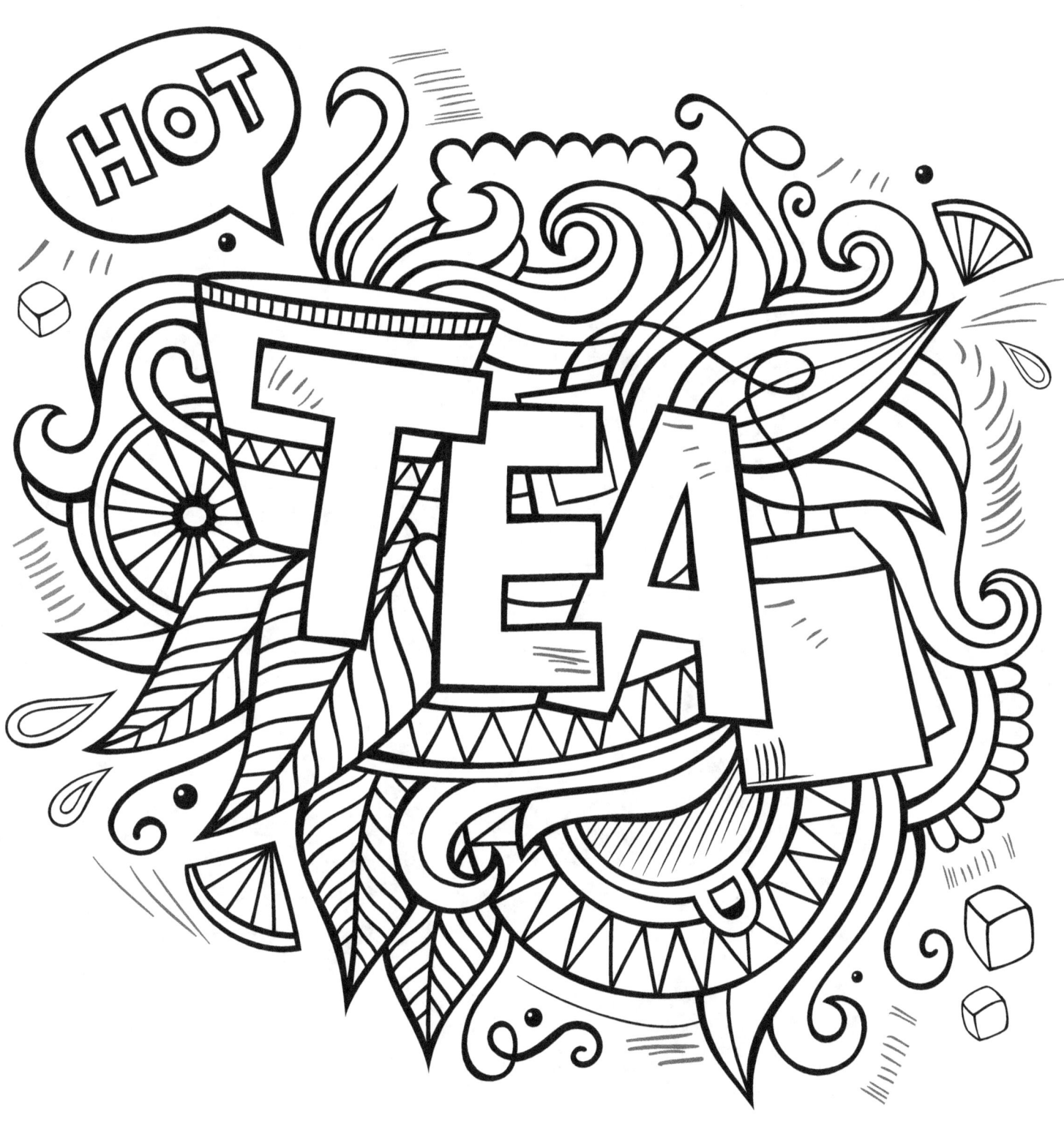

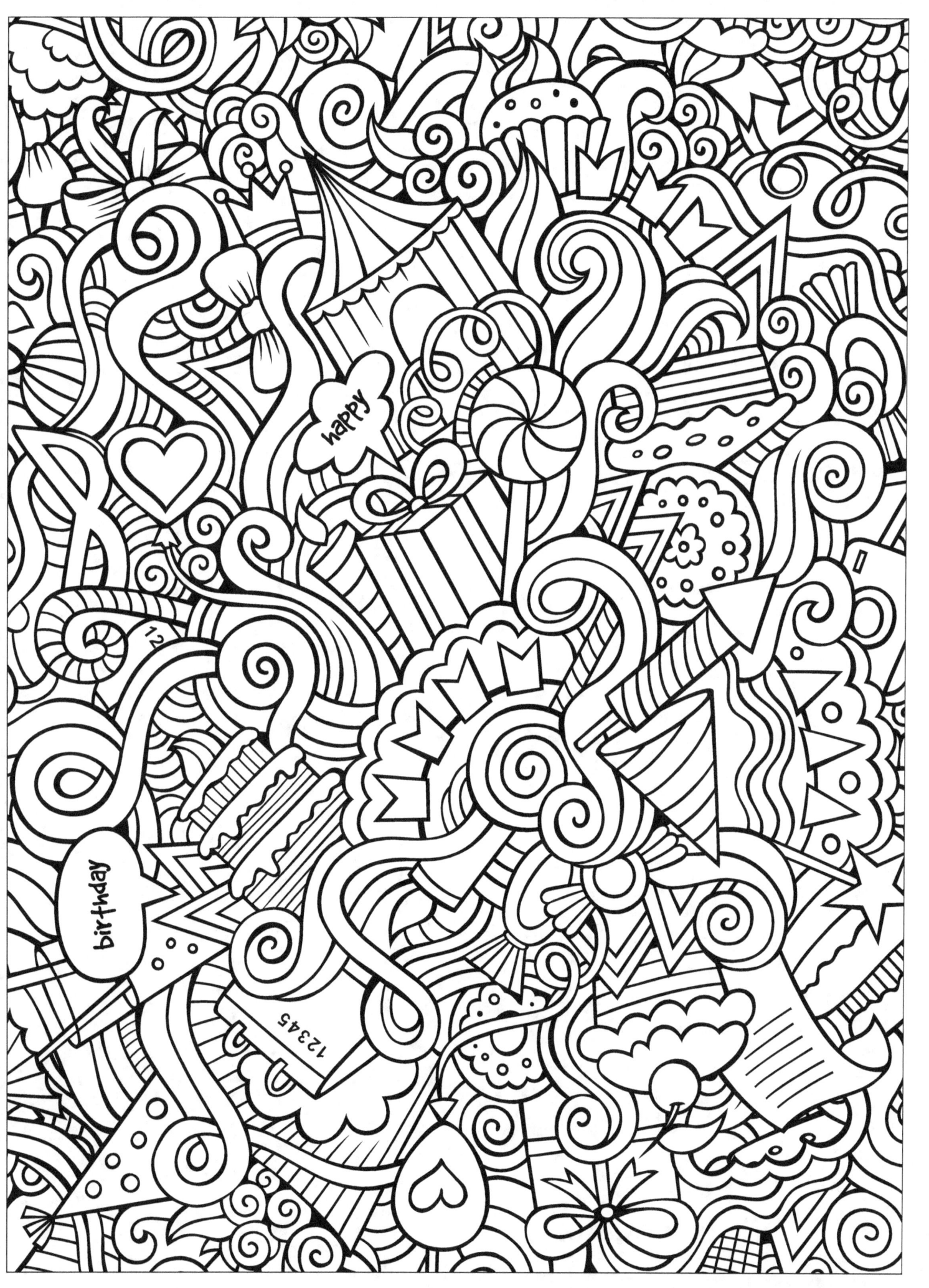

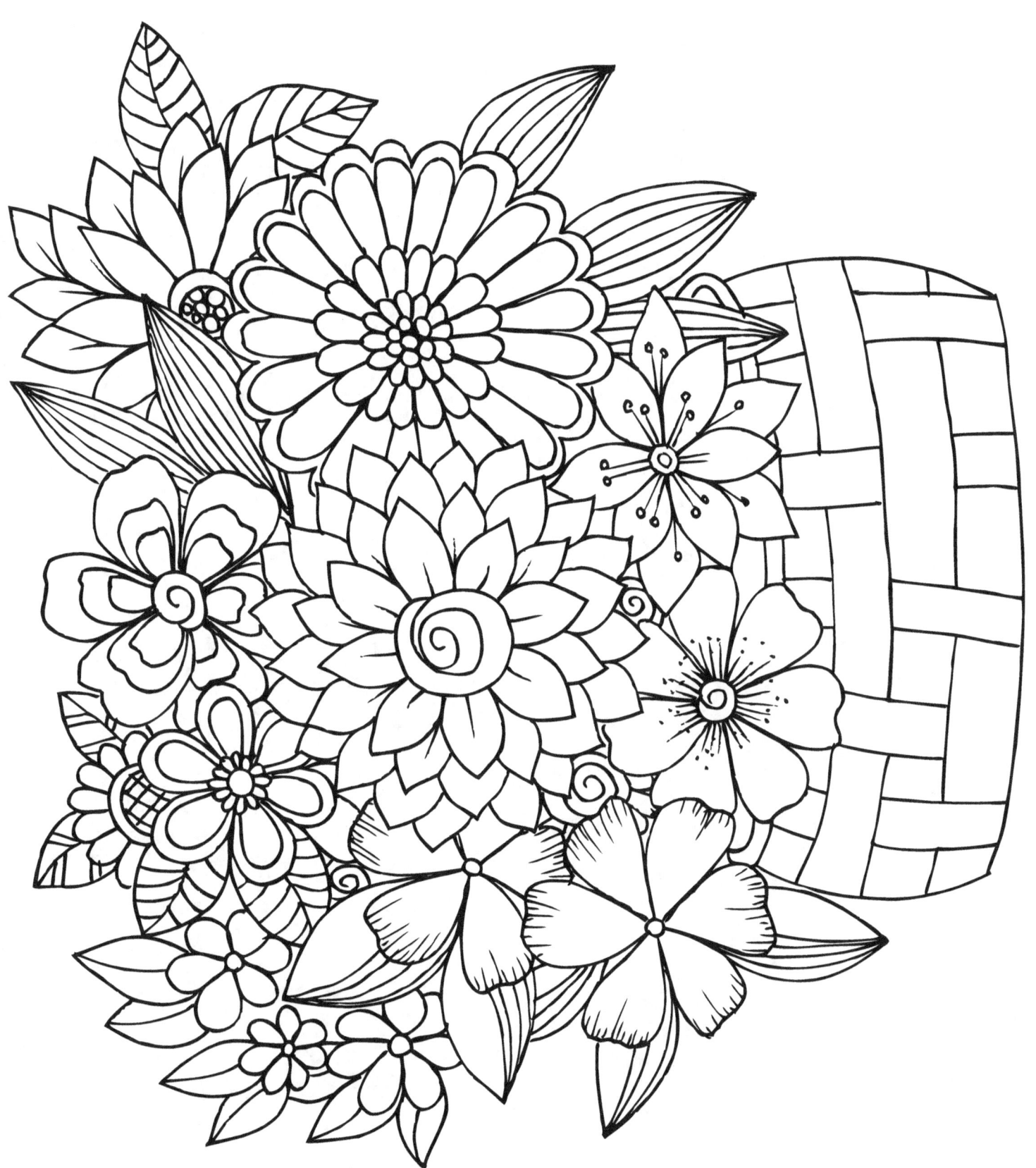

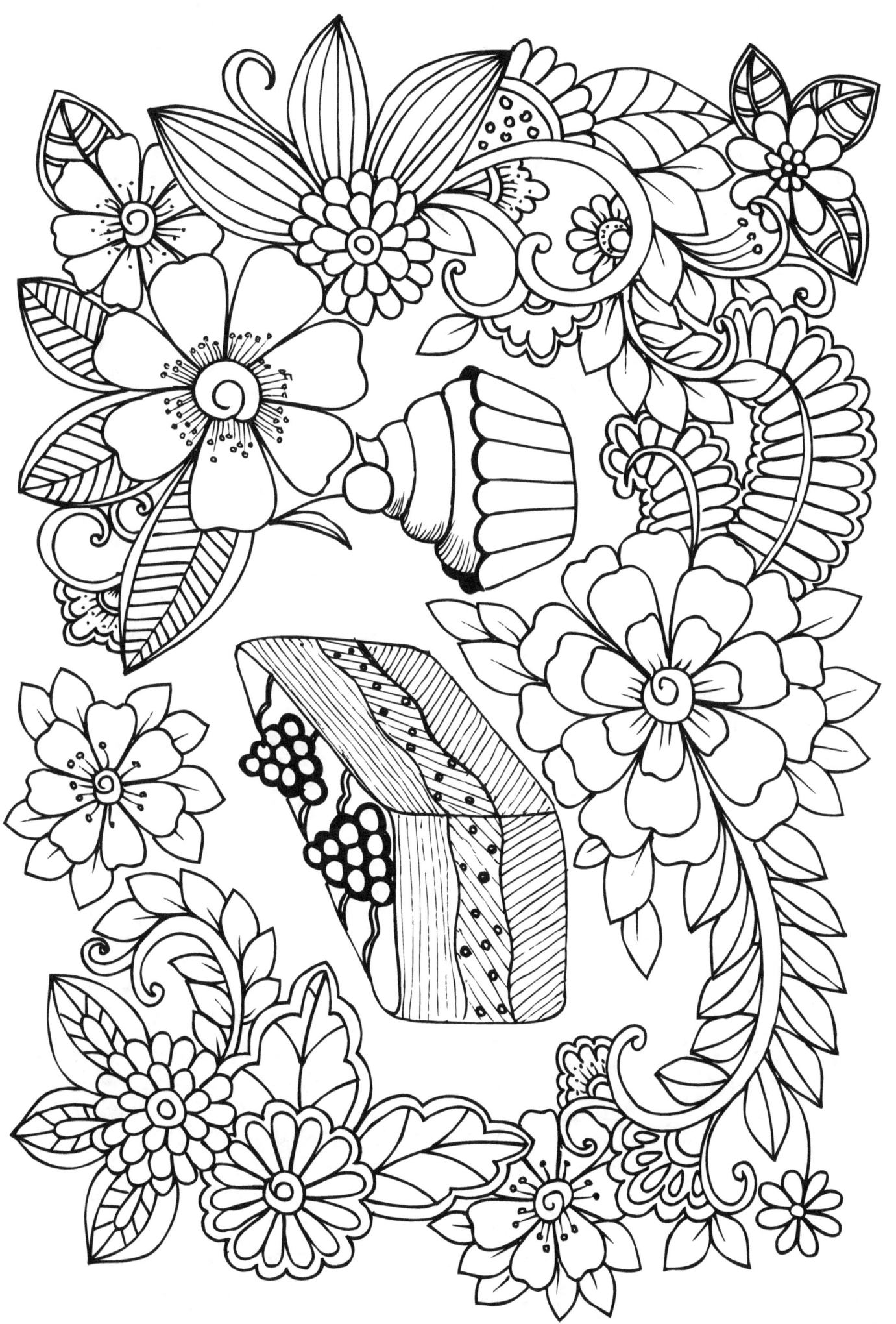

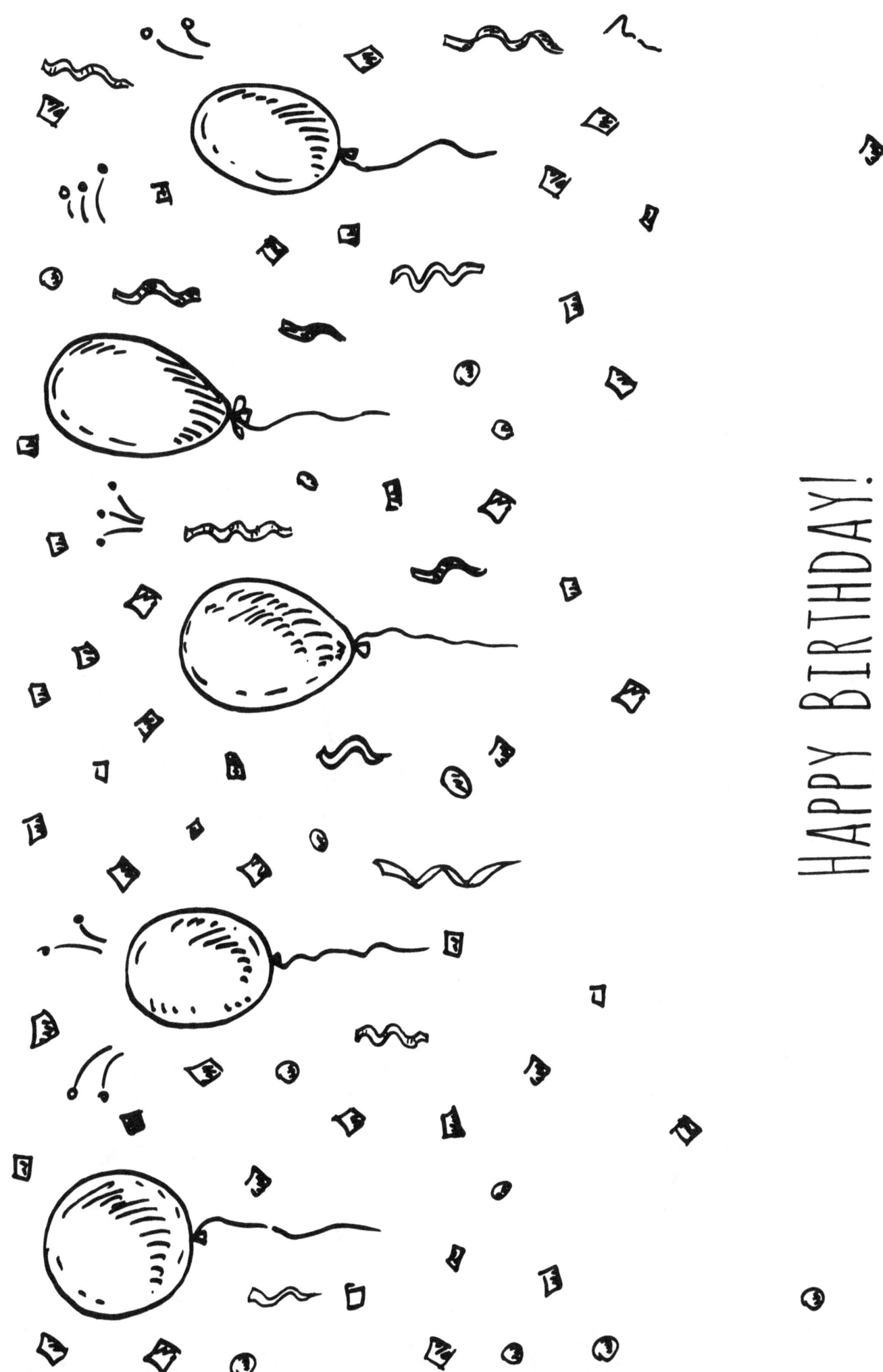

Happy Birthday!

Best Selling Art Therapy Coloring Books

Coloring Books For Adults:

- Zombie Coloring Book: Black Background
- Butterfly Coloring Book For Adults: Black Background
- Tattoo Coloring Book: Black Background
- Coloring Books for Adults Relaxation: Native American Inspired Designs
- Fishing Coloring Book for Adults: Black Background

Coloring Books For Men:

- Coloring Book for Men: Anti-Stress Designs Vol 1
- Coloring Book For Men: Fishing Designs
- Coloring Book For Men: Tattoo Designs
- Coloring Books for Men: Hunting
- Coloring Book For Men: Biker Designs

Coloring Books For Seniors:

- Coloring Book For Seniors: Nature Designs Vol 1
- Coloring Book For Seniors: Anti-Stress Designs Vol 1
- Coloring Books for Seniors: Relaxing Designs
- Coloring Book For Seniors: Floral Designs Vol 1
- Coloring Book For Seniors: Ocean Designs Vol 1

Coloring Books For Teens and Tweens:

- Coloring Books For Teens: Ocean Designs
- Coloring Books for Teen Girls Vol 1
- Teen Inspirational Coloring Books
- Coloring Book for Teens: Anti-Stress Designs Vol 1
- Tween Coloring Books For Girls: Cute Animals

Coloring Books For Kids:

- Horse Coloring Book For Girls
- Coloring Books For Boys: Sharks
- Coloring Books for Boys: Animal Designs
- Unicorn Coloring Book for Girls
- Detailed Coloring Books For Kids

Coloring Books For Adults

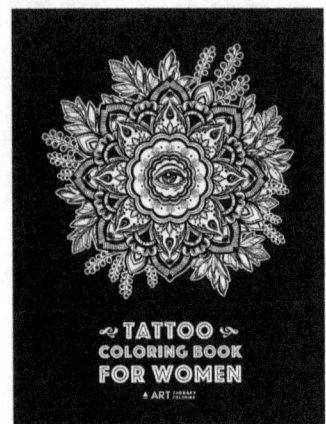

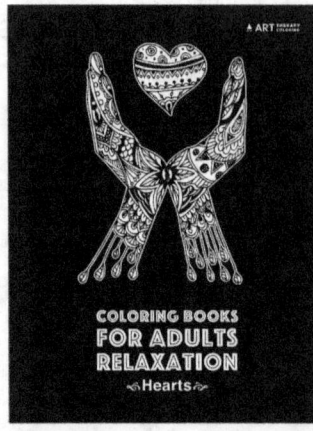

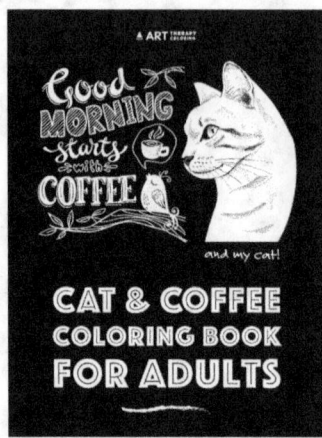

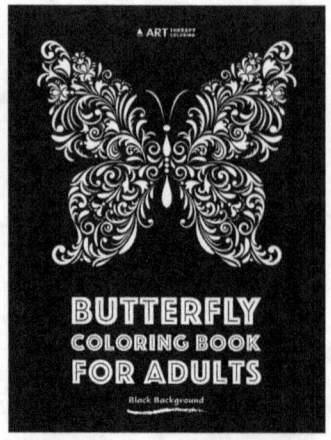

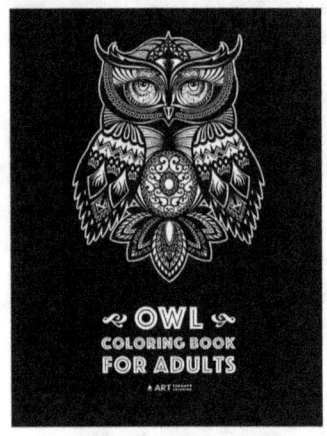

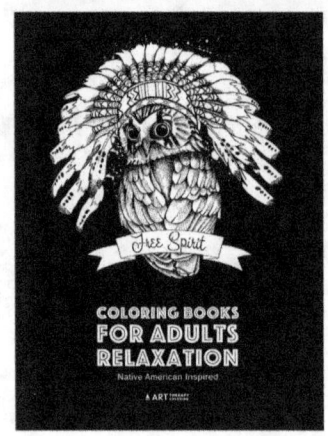

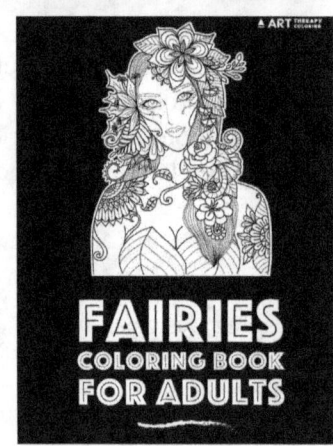

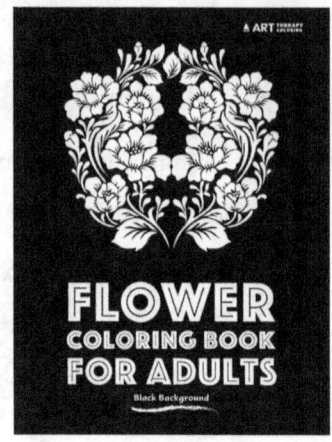

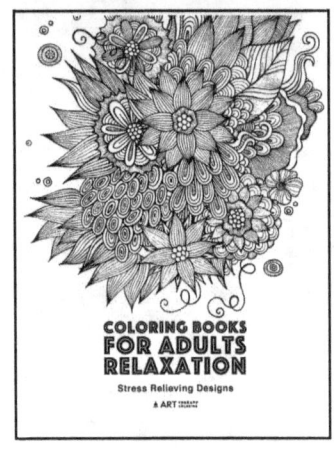

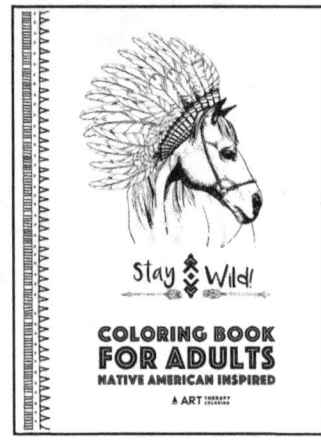

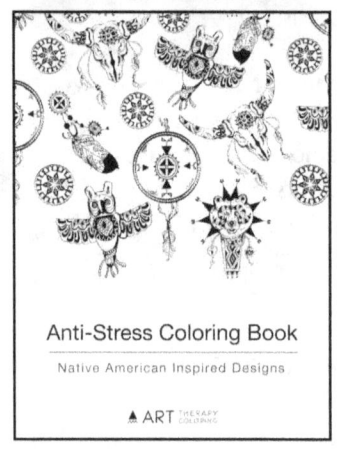

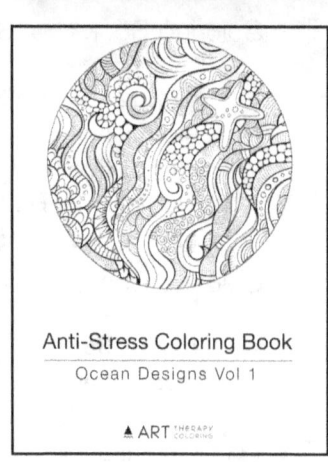

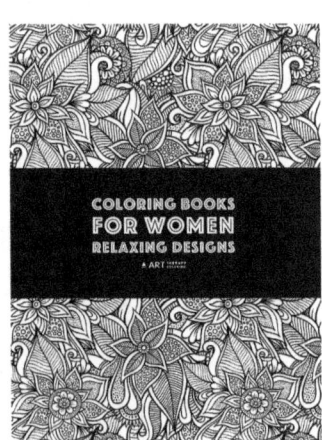

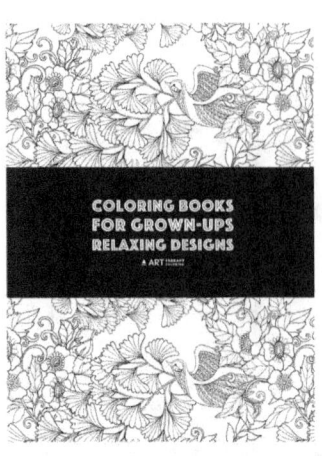

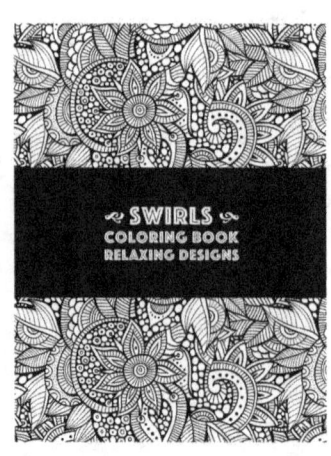

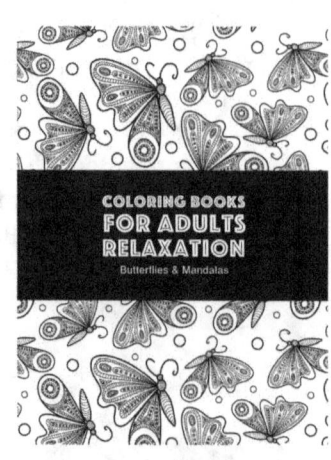

Coloring Books For Adults

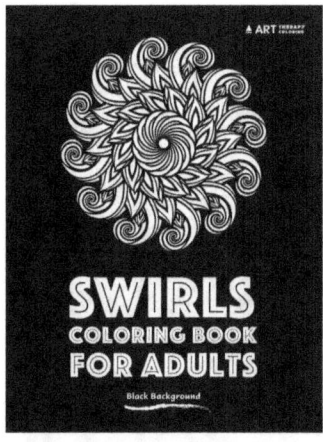

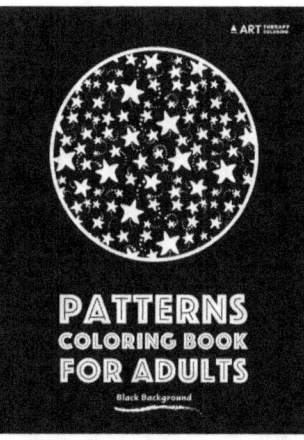

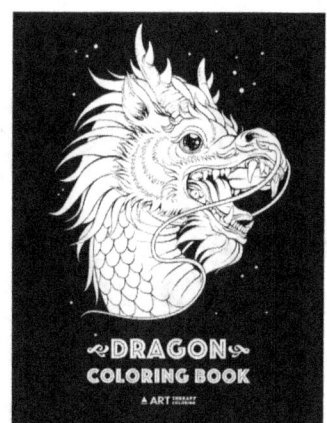

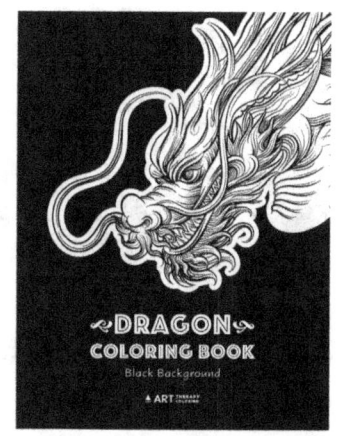

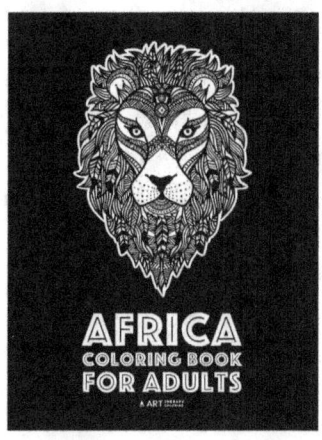

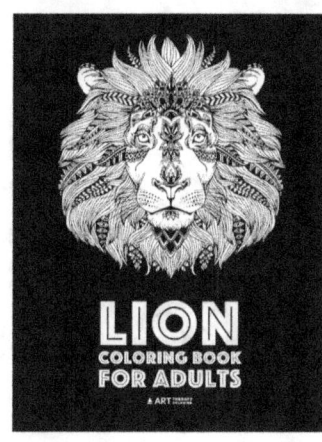

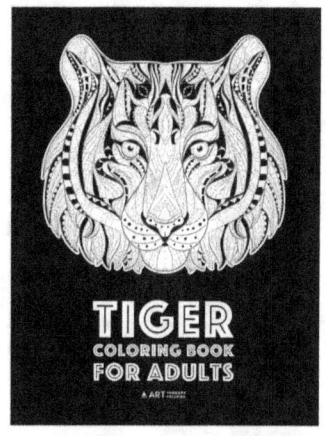

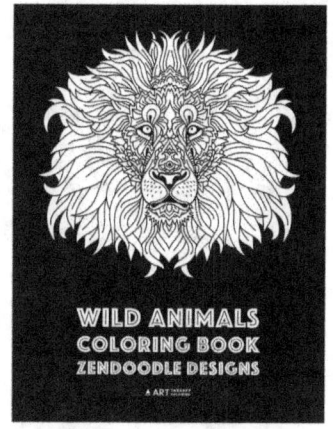

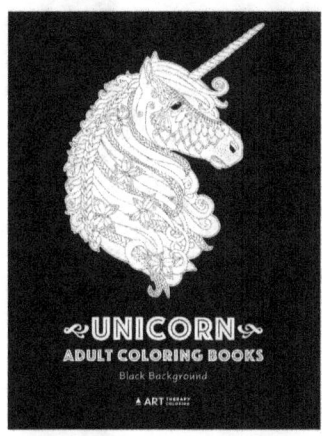

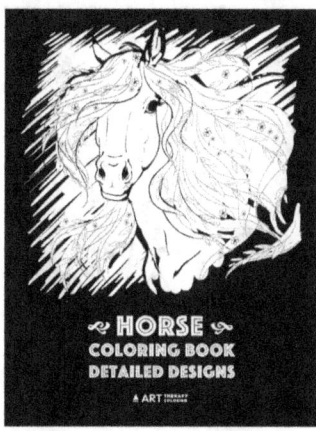

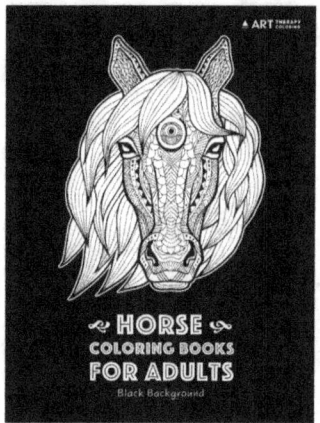

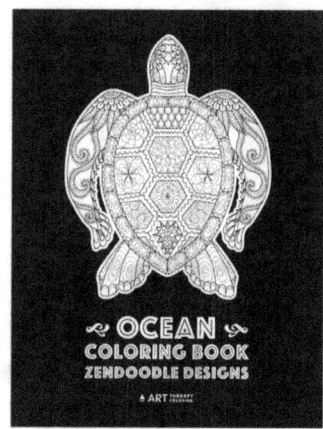

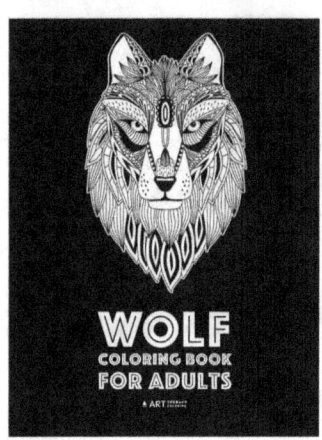

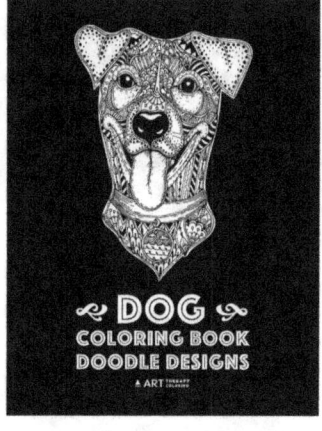

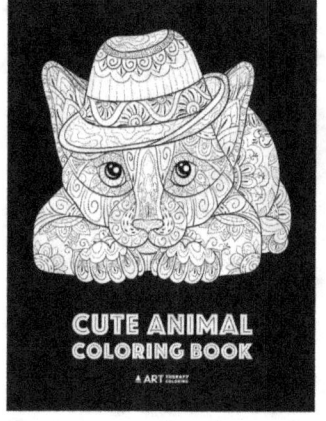

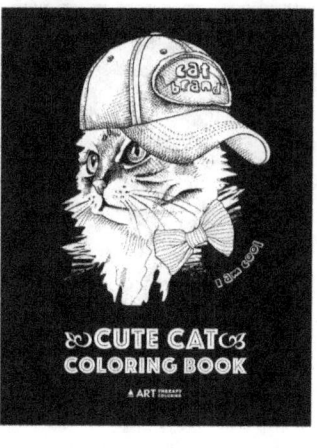

Coloring Books For Teens

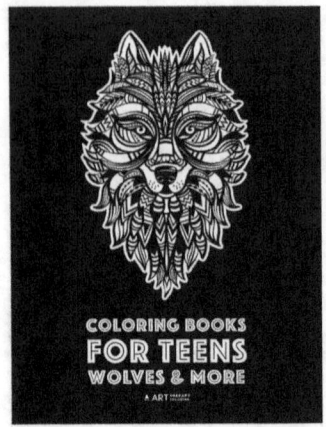

COLORING BOOKS FOR TEENS WOLVES & MORE

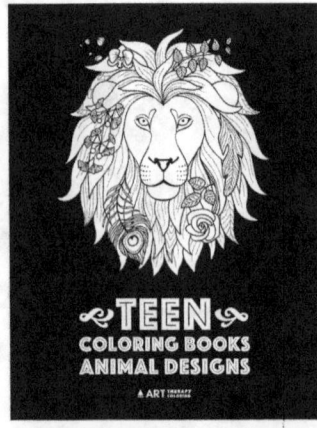

TEEN COLORING BOOKS ANIMAL DESIGNS

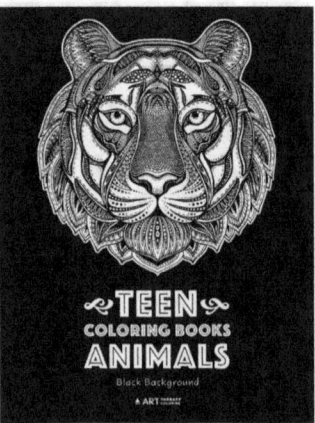

TEEN COLORING BOOKS ANIMALS
Black Background

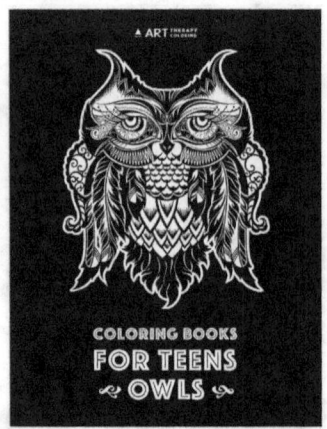

COLORING BOOKS FOR TEENS OWLS

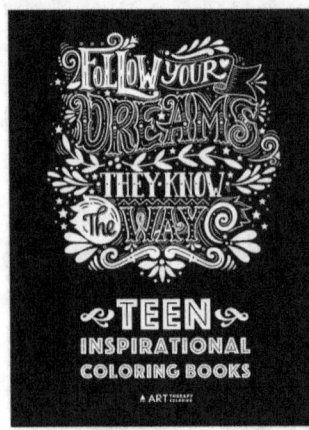

TEEN INSPIRATIONAL COLORING BOOKS

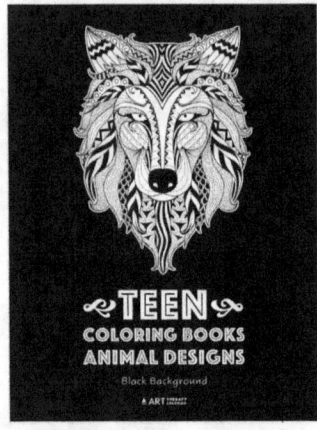

TEEN COLORING BOOKS ANIMAL DESIGNS
Black Background

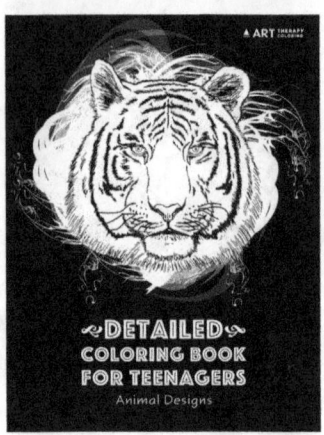

DETAILED COLORING BOOK FOR TEENAGERS
Animal Designs

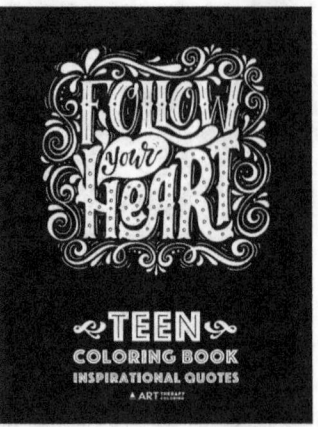

TEEN COLORING BOOK INSPIRATIONAL QUOTES

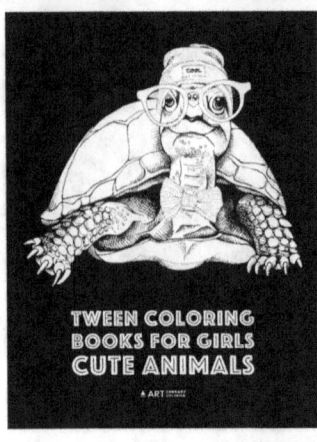

TWEEN COLORING BOOKS FOR GIRLS CUTE ANIMALS

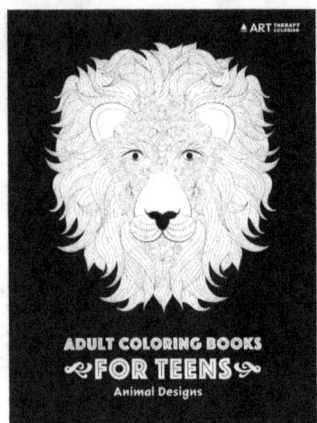

ADULT COLORING BOOKS FOR TEENS
Animal Designs

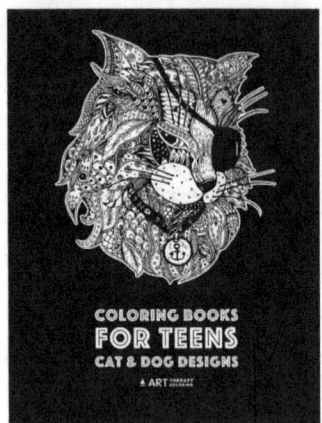

COLORING BOOKS FOR TEENS CAT & DOG DESIGNS

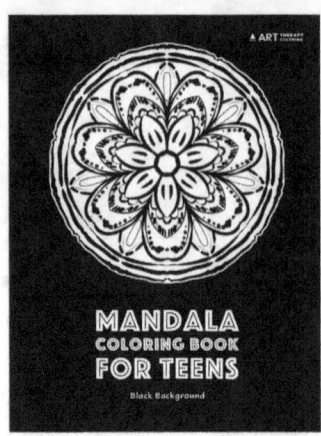

MANDALA COLORING BOOK FOR TEENS
Black Background

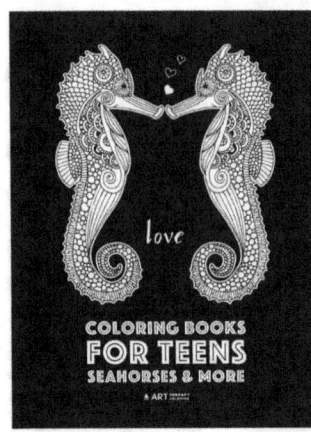

COLORING BOOKS FOR TEENS SEAHORSES & MORE

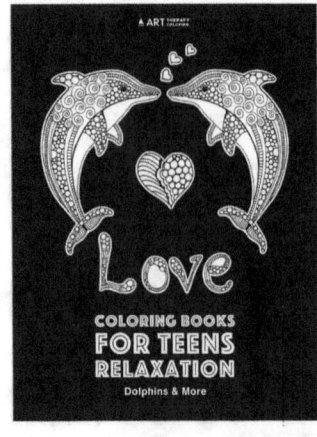

COLORING BOOKS FOR TEENS RELAXATION
Dolphins & More

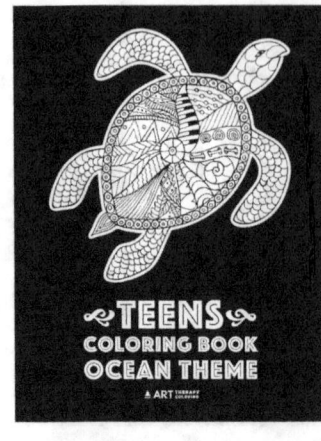

TEENS COLORING BOOK OCEAN THEME

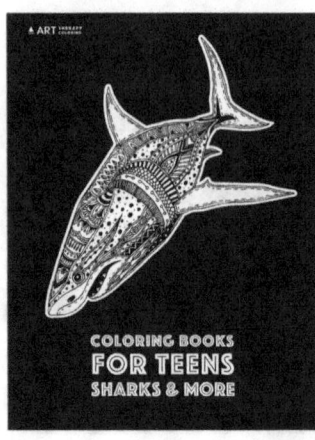

COLORING BOOKS FOR TEENS SHARKS & MORE

Coloring Books For Teens

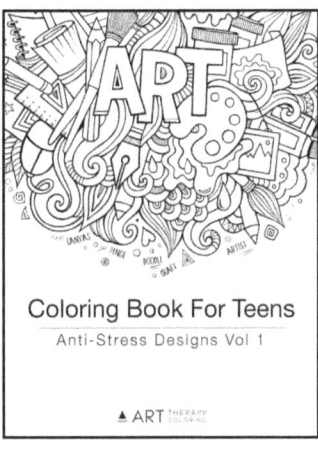

Coloring Book For Teens
Anti-Stress Designs Vol 1
ART THERAPY COLORING

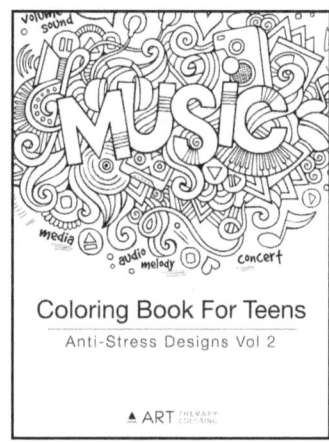

Coloring Book For Teens
Anti-Stress Designs Vol 2
ART THERAPY COLORING

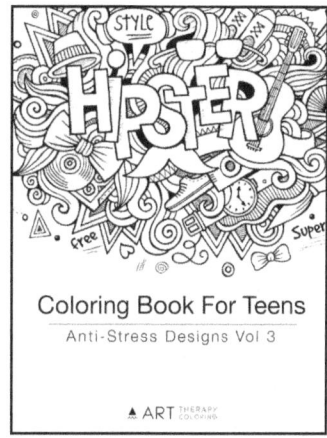

Coloring Book For Teens
Anti-Stress Designs Vol 3
ART THERAPY COLORING

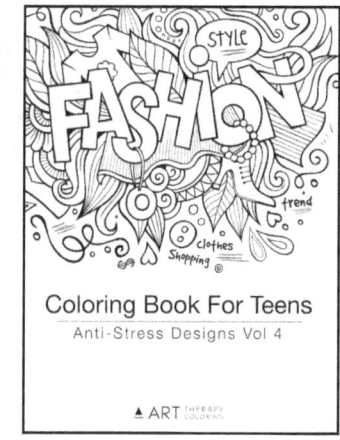

Coloring Book For Teens
Anti-Stress Designs Vol 4
ART THERAPY COLORING

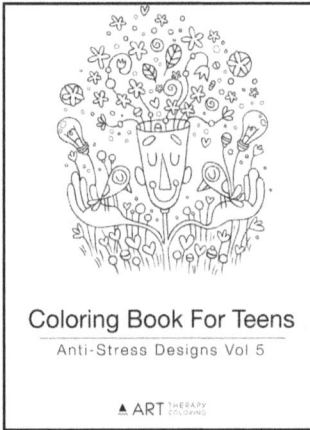

Coloring Book For Teens
Anti-Stress Designs Vol 5
ART THERAPY COLORING

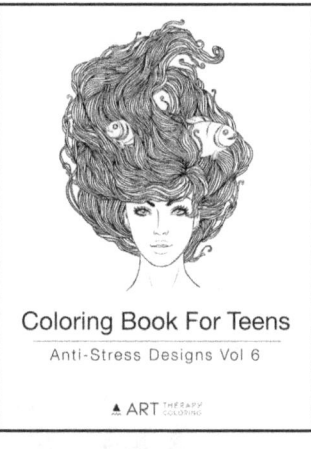

Coloring Book For Teens
Anti-Stress Designs Vol 6
ART THERAPY COLORING

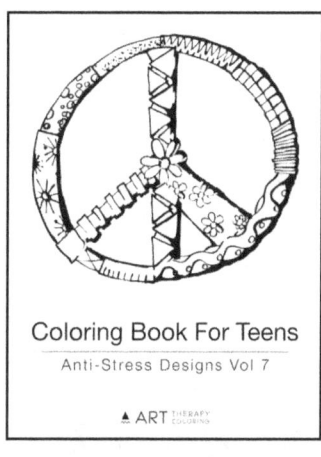

Coloring Book For Teens
Anti-Stress Designs Vol 7
ART THERAPY COLORING

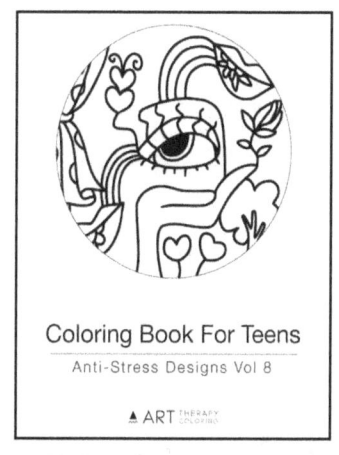

Coloring Book For Teens
Anti-Stress Designs Vol 8
ART THERAPY COLORING

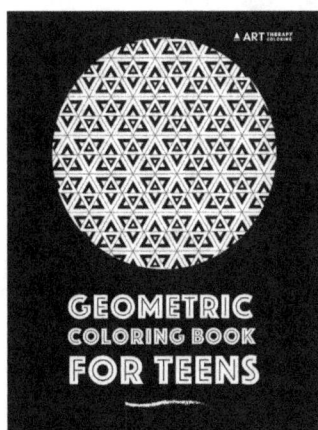

GEOMETRIC COLORING BOOK FOR TEENS

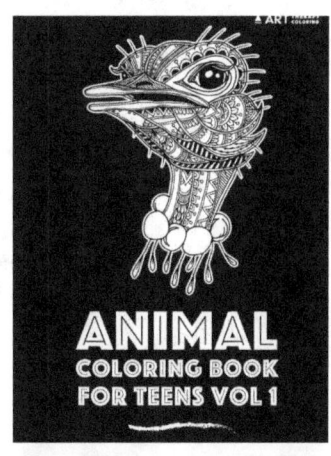

ANIMAL COLORING BOOK FOR TEENS VOL 1

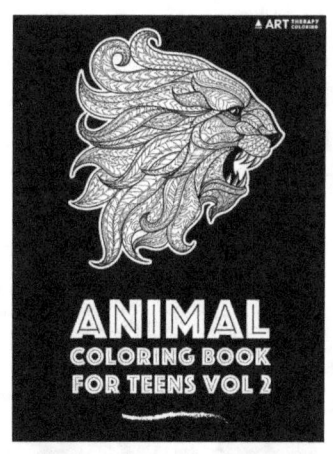

ANIMAL COLORING BOOK FOR TEENS VOL 2

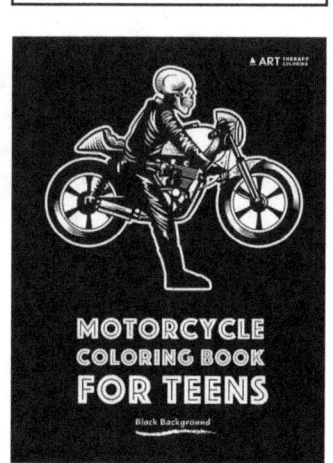

MOTORCYCLE COLORING BOOK FOR TEENS
Black Background

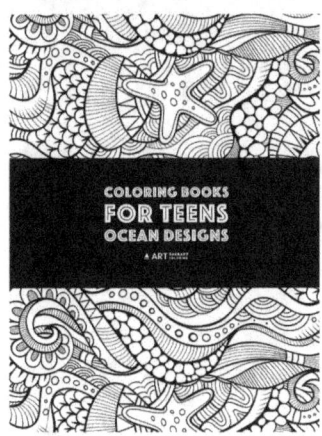

COLORING BOOKS FOR TEENS OCEAN DESIGNS
ART THERAPY COLORING

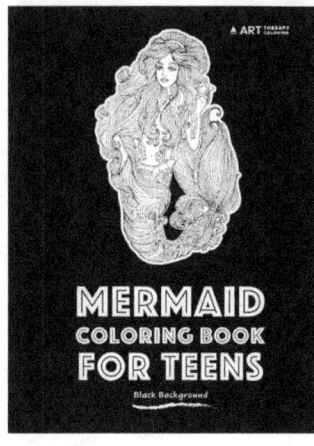

MERMAID COLORING BOOK FOR TEENS
Black Background

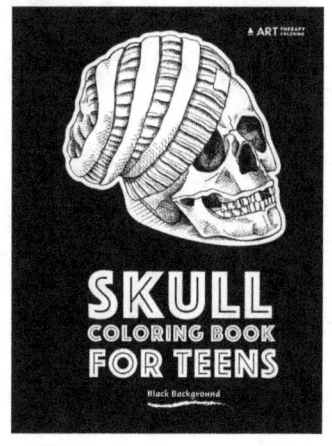

SKULL COLORING BOOK FOR TEENS
Black Background

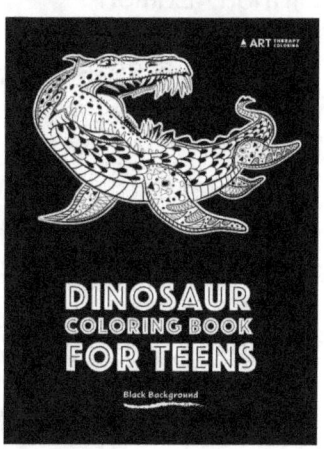

DINOSAUR COLORING BOOK FOR TEENS
Black Background

Anti-Stress Coloring Book
Birthday Edition

Published by:
Art Therapy Coloring
www.arttherapycoloring.com

Images Under License From Shutterstock

ISBN: 978-1-944427-01-6